NOON DAY SUN

Cassandra Medley

BROADWAY PLAY PUBLISHING INC
224 E 62nd St, NY, NY 10065
www.broadwayplaypub.com
info@broadwayplaypub.com

NOON DAY SUN
© Copyright 2006 by Cassandra Medley

First printing: February 2007
I S B N: 0-88145-322-6

Book design: Marie Donovan
Word processing: Microsoft Word
Typographic controls: Ventura Publisher
Typeface: Palatino
Printed and bound in the U S A

ORIGINAL PRODUCTION

The world premiere of NOON DAY SUN was
produced at the TheaterFest Theater (Geoffrey
Newman, Producer), Montclair NJ in June 2001.
The cast and creative contributor were:

ZENA .... Gin Hammond
BRIAN .... Karl Kenzler
LLOYD ....Peter Davis
REUBEN .... Gregory Simmons
CONJURE WOMAN ....Akonke Nur
PEARL ....Melanie Nicholls-King

Director .... John Wooten

CHARACTERS & SETTING

ZENA, *a very fair skinned black woman in her late twenties, early thirties*

REUBEN, *a brown skinned black man, in his thirties*

BRIAN, *white man, early thirties*

PEARL, *a dark skinned black woman in her late twenties, early thirties*

MISS ETTA, *an elderly black Negro conjure woman*
SISTER NICODEMOS, *a middle aged black woman*
BERTHA, *a middle aged black woman*
MIDWIFE, *a middle aged black woman*
these characters can be played by the same actress.

LLOYD, *a white, middle aged business man*
POLICEMAN
TRAIN CONDUCTOR
these characters can be played by the same actor

Time and Place: A muggy week in Detroit, Michigan, September, 1957, and various points in ZENA's *past.*

Set pieces should be minimal, the intent is to use lights and sounds to suggest the various scenes.

SPECIAL THANKS

First and foremost to: Meir Ribalow and the New River Dramatists. To Patricia Randell, Leslie Ann Carol, and Gin Hammond, for helping to "birth" Zena. To Melanie Nicholls-King for Pearl. To Akonke Nur, Peter Davies, and Gregory Simmons.

To John Wooten for his vision and faith in the script.

To Kathleen Hill, Jennifer Wortham, Betsy and Dorsey McConnell, David Williams, and L-R Berger, and Eileen Guzmich, as always.

ACT ONE

Scene One

(A summer morning, 1947)

(Suddenly the sound of a train whistle. A train
CONDUCTOR's *voice in Southern drawl, rings out.* ZENA
mimes boarding a train. The train CONDUCTOR, *stands in*
the shadows dressed in the traditional cap and jacket, with his
back towards the audience)

CONDUCTOR: All ee-board!! Seven A M local for
Collinsville, Natchez, Greenwhood, change at
Greenwood for the express to Indianola...all other
passengers stay on board for Ox-ford and Memphis,
all ee-board please!! Tickets!! Tickets ready please—
tickets!!!

(Spotlight comes up on ZENA. *She is in a simple country*
dress, standing in spotlight holding a battered suitcase.)

ZENA: ...That morning...already so hot. Already a
noon-day sun and not even eight o'clock...heat like
a torch in your face that won't go out... *(Pause)* All it
took was for me to step up to the platform, climb them
three iron steps...somebody's hands already helping me
with my..."our"...suitcase, swinging it on the rack above
my head. Seats so full for that time of early morning...
all sorts of Colored faces all headed to Memphis or, like
me, points further North...families crowded in together,
ropes holding their few belongings inside overstuffed
boxes...smells of cold fried chicken, wrapped in oilskin,

made the night before...faces friendly...smiling folks...Colored people headed for...paradise up "North"...

(CONDUCTOR's *voice booms out.*)

CONDUCTOR: Tickets!! Tickets ready please!! Tickets!!

(ZENA *holds out her hand as if offering a ticket. She extends her hand in an offering gesture*)

ZENA: I always thought that when, and if God was to ever come to test us, that it would be...I dunno—well, like some moment full of thunder...some flash of brightness striking you blind in the face, like Reverend Thomas preached about St. Paul struck down on his way to Damascus... *(Pause)* But no...when it finally does happen? It can be so simple, so quiet. See, God can slip a "test" right in-between your breath, and you not even know till you're looking back from behind you.

CONDUCTOR: Tickets!!

(ZENA *holds her ticket out.*)

(CONDUCTOR *tips his hat to* ZENA.)

CONDUCTOR: 'Cuse me, M'am, but you done made a terrible mistake....

ZENA: "Mistake"? But my ticket's paid in full! Is this the wrong train? I'm headed for Memphis and due North...what...is there some...

CONDUCTOR: Naw, naw, pretty Miss, don't get excited. But this here's the nigger coach, ain't you noticed it? You want the car up front that's reserved for our white clientele, follow me...right this way...

(*The* CONDUCTOR *politely removes* ZENA's *country dress, revealing a stylish summer cocktail dress underneath.*)

ZENA: And there it was. God's test so fast, so easy, so...surprising and simple, I barely had a moment to

feel myself taking in air. Handed my "magic carpet"
by some red-faced, pug-nosed fool who was "doing his
duty" for the purity of his race. Ha. *(Pause)* Felt like I
was moving and standing still at the same time. He
lifted my suitcase for me like I was the genuine lady he
believed me to be. *(Pause)* And I walked down that aisle
past all the rest of us Colored...watching me in silence...
past the smirks on their faces...past eyes...and if
bitterness could cut they would have slashed me.
(She puts on stylish earrings and necklace. Pause) Well, I
just keep walking forward...straight ahead...and from
that day to this I never look behind, I just keep walking.

(Lights immediately change to ten years later)

Scene Two

(The Present, ten years later—July, 1957)

(A ballroom in Detroit Michigan)

*(The reception. Laughter and crowd noise. Smatterings of
blurred conversations. ZENA is speaking confidently to an
unseen companion.)*

ZENA: *(Laughing)* Nunno—when I say, "brown"
—I'm talking about velvety, caramel-colored,
lick-your-lips "brown." Smooth. A caramel ribbon,
folding on your plate. Blend in the flour...keep the
flame low...never stop stirring, blending...roast your
giblets along "with" the turkey, then remove each piece
as it gets tender... trust me. Your Mister'll grovel at your
feet, ha. *(Listens for a reply, then)* M'dear anything out
the "box" or "can" is fake, win him over with gen-iu-
ine Southern-style gravy that's come down through
generations! *(Points suddenly)* There's your Mister
looking for you. *(Calls out)* Freddie, here she is, over
here! *(To unseen companion)* Go on over—go 'head,
we'll all make a foursome at dinner tonight...then

there's dancing... So, lovely to meet you, Betty, aren't
you so sweet—
remember now—all this week it's our duty as the wives
to "play-play-play..." *(She waves as the unseen companion
moves off. A moment as she sips from her drink and smiles
confidently, glancing around.)*

(Enter BRIAN, *dressed in a formal suit and carrying martinis)*

BRIAN: *(As in a whisper to* ZENA*)* I wanna pour this
down your dress.

ZENA: Shame on you. Bad boy.

BRIAN: *(Whispering)* Punish me tonight.

*(*ZENA *giggles. Then they both switch into formal, sociable
smiles, reaching their hands out to shake with unseen couples
who pass by)*

BRIAN: Hi, there! *(Indicating himself and* ZENA*)* I'm Brian
Syms from Patterson Manufacturing Inc., Fort Wayne,
Indiana, and this is my wife, Wendy.

ZENA: *(Offering her hand, smiling)* Hullo. ...Yes, this is
our first time, too, and we're really looking forward to
it.

BRIAN: *(Responding to comment)* ...Right, you are there.
Just let us at the big-boys so we can sell our "wares"
—know what I mean?

ZENA: ...Mrs Supino, if you don't mind my saying
that is the smartest hat I'm seen all afternoon... *(Pause)*
Why you're welcome. See you both at the dinner-dance.

*(*ZENA *and* BRIAN *wave as the couple moves off.)*

BRIAN: *(Whispering to* ZENA*)* I wanna pour this down
your dress and lick you all over

ZENA: *(Laughing)* Behave, you're in public

BRIAN: Can't help myself.

ZENA: Pretend to behave, then.

BRIAN: What'd you think I'm doing? *(Pause)* I adore you.

ZENA: Tell me twice.

BRIAN: I...

(Suddenly lights swirl and glitter as band music begins, a drum roll is heard and then ANNOUNCER's *voice)*

ANNOUNCER: *(Off-stage, Jackie Gleason style)* Huh-ba... huh-ba...huh-ba... Welcome everybody and Hoodie-doodie-doo—Welcome to Detroit-City, the Motor Capital of the World and our spectacular "Autorama" Nineteen Fifty—Seven!!!

(Thunderous applause, ZENA *and* BRIAN *clap wildly along with the rest, as the band music and conversation continues.)*

*(*LLOYD *appears as if out of nowhere, kissing* ZENA's *hand, back-slapping* BRIAN.)*

LLOYD: *(He takes her face in his hands.)* And is *this* the face that'll launch a thousand ships this week, eh?

BRIAN: Mister Davis.

ZENA: *(To* LLOYD*)* Oh, I'm ready, willing and able to "launch" whatever it takes to help my "one-and-only."

LLOYD: Spoken like a true, blue, company gal. And if I know anything, she'll be the Belle of the Auto-rama by this evening...

ZENA: Aren't you sweet, Mister Davis, so sweet.

LLOYD: Lloyd. After all we're all here on business holiday.

ZENA: Lloyd. *(Pause)* You keep on wearing smokey-grey ties to match your eyes- and—heaven help us when the word gets out you a widower and all—I just don't think I'm gonna be able to hold the women off.

BRIAN: *(Embarrassed)* Honey!

LLOYD: Nunno-no—leave her be—I swear, Mrs Syms if you aren't the—the *(Speechless, charmed)* —oh, boy, oh boy.

BRIAN: You should've seen her on the plane, sir. Knew all the Western Division wives by name by the time we landed. Now, that's my girl.

LLOYD: *(To ZENA)* Well, you've got the whole Fort Wayne division of Patterson under your spell, let's see you "lay waste" to Detroit.

ZENA: Oh, but what I couldn't get over is how they all kinda dismiss the strategic importance of our Fort Wayne plant—oooh, I just got so mad!

LLOYD: *(Patting her cheek)* You? *(Chuckles)* Impossible. Y'might as well try to keep the sun from shining.

ZENA: Bri spent the whole entire flight setting 'em all straight.

BRIAN: That's what he's brought me here for, darlin.

LLOYD: Damn tootin. *(Patting his back)* This here's m'new hot-shot Boy. *(Looks out over the "crowd")* Lookit 'em all—Western, Midwestern, Eastern, Southern, Canadian...all with their up-and-coming "star sluggers" at the ready.

ZENA: *(To LLOYD)* But you two are gonna beat 'em out—and Ford, and Chryslers, and G M are gonna contract out for plate glass and car parts to us back in Fort Wayne, Indie...

LLOYD: *(Kissing her hand)* Now-now, no need to let stuffy-ole business matters worry your pretty self. I'd always tell my beloved Madeline, God rest her, "just shine and let us fella do the work, just shine".

BRIAN: I've been trying to tell her that, sir.

LLOYD: Lloyd.

BRIAN: Yes, sir. Besides, she'll probably soon have more "domestic" concerns to concentrate on very soon. *(He pecks her cheek)*

ZENA: *(Abruptly pointing)* Mister and Mrs Charles Wallace out of Kansas City. Lloyd, I told them all about your home-grown orchids—they wanna meet you.

LLOYD: *(Moving off)* Secret's in the fertilizer, the right blend... *(He disappears,)*

ZENA: *(Whirling on* BRIAN, *referring to* LLOYD*)* Please, don't tease me like that.

BRIAN: Whoa—hold it—

ZENA: You promised.

BRIAN: *(Making peace)* Hey. Look around. *(Gesturing towards the crowd)* We've come a long, long way for a couple of night school loners huh?

ZENA: And, I *adore* you.

(A drum roll)

ANNOUNCER: *(Off-stage)* And now—the moment we've all been waiting for—let's have a big hand for the look, the style, the comfort of the brand, new, 1958 Chev-ro-let!

(BRIAN *and* ZENA *clap along with the crowd with smiling, then turn to each other.)*

BRIAN: How'd I ever end up with the "Princess of the Ball"?

(A discrete kiss)

ZENA: *(Pointing to the crowd)* Look at 'em... None have your guts. None of 'em know what it is to scrape up from the bottom. They're all still little boys playing at matches.

BRIAN: More champagne? *(He takes* ZENA's *glass, and disappears into the shadows.)*

(Dina Shore's piped in voice sings: See the U S A in Your Chevrolet/America's the greatest land of all....*)*

(Clapping as a twirling spotlight beaming from off stage signals the new car being unveiled for display. More clapping and crowd "ooos" and "ahhs." Ballroom music resumes.)

(Enter REUBEN, *a black janitor in his early thirties, dressed in an olive green uniform, pushing a broom cluttered with confetti. He stops suddenly, watching from the shadows.)*

*(*REUBEN *very slowly positions himself so as to catch* ZENA's *eye. She sees him, her smile freezes on her face.)*

(From the shadows Ms ETTA, *an elderly Black Woman enters, an apparition unseen by* BRIAN *or* REUBEN. *She is draped in necklaces of animal bones, She shakes her necklace and the music stops, she locks eyes with* ZENA.*)*

ETTA: Don't you wanna know what the "bones" say? Don't you wanna know? *(She disappears.)*

(Lights cross fade. The ballroom music resumes but muffled as if from a distance.)

*(*ZENA *and* REUBEN *step down or up onto another platform.* REUBEN *takes out a large ring of keys and mimes unlocking a door. He furtively glances behind as* ZENA *follows him from a distance. They lock eyes, and enter what should seem to be a tight closet. He mimes locking the door.)*

(Faint voice of off-stage ANNOUNCER *is heard in the distance)*

ANNOUNCER: *(Off-stage. From a distance)* Here she is, folks—the Nineteen Fifty-Eight Oldsmobile..!

(Faint off-stage applause as REUBEN *and* ZENA *stand in silence, staring at each other.)*

REUBEN: *(Pause)* Welcome to my supply closet in the "Motor capital of the world."

(Silence. They stare at each other.)

ZENA: I don't believe... *(Stops)*

REUBEN: Maybe I'm a mirage.

ZENA: *(A beat)* They do say the world's a tiny place.

REUBEN: Shrinking all the time.

ZENA: You.

REUBEN: *(Pause)* Dang. *(Beat)* You. Got prettier.

ZENA: You're. Looking fit.

REUBEN: *(Indicates himself)* Stopped swilling that rot-gut liquor. Been free of the "juice" ten years.

ZENA: Guess miracles "do" happen.

REUBEN: Is that what "this" is?

ZENA: *(Scoffing)* Talk sense.

(Silence, she just stares at him.)

REUBEN: So. What you tell your "rumba man"? Huh? That you had to go "powder your nose"?

ZENA: When'd you leave from down there?

REUBEN: Dog-gone it, you *would* go and get prettier.

ZENA: How long you been in Detroit?

REUBEN: *(Shrugs)* Hey, the Motor City's where the "hip cats" be happening, baby.

ZENA: Oh, Lord, so you're talking "jive" like all these other street hustling Negroes.

REUBEN: What you want me talking? Nigga talk? Sharecropping talk? "Yessir Massa" talk? *(Beat)* Ain't that a bitch. Ten years and you "fine as wine and the grapes off the vine."

(They stare at each other.)

REUBEN: Played "7-7-7" from the "dream book" yesterday, too. Book said something "highly unusual" was set to happen. *(Silence)*

ZENA: Did you sneak off the place?

REUBEN: *(Mocking)* Naw. Boss Man McClellan say, "Reuben Sinclair? Never mind that ton of debt you got, lemme throw you a *'bon voyage'* party!" *(Pause)* Hopped me a freight the fall of '49—just after the harvest. Everybody claimed up North here was "Paradise."

ZENA: Why not go to Chicago—isn't the "blues" big in Chicago?

REUBEN: Let that ole pipe dream gather dust. *(Pause)* So. *This* what happened to ya.

ZENA: *(Indicating his uniform)* How long have you been working in this place?

REUBEN: Long enough to get "lucky" today, I reckon.

ZENA: *(Moving to leave)* Well—. Take care of yourself. Bye.

REUBEN: Is he Wop or Mick? Looks "Mick" to me.

ZENA: I had every right to cut out on you.

REUBEN: Who's saying any different.

ZENA: Drunk every day God sent! Juking every joint in the County. Blubbering over that guitar. Leaving *us* each and every night! ...Leaving our fields to rot.

REUBEN: "Mister Charlie's" fields.

ZENA: Fields we ate from, whose ever they were!

(He takes one of his rags and waves it like a flag of "truce".)

REUBEN: So. Where you and Mister Peckerwood living at?

ZENA: The main thing is, I *am* living.

REUBEN: Gal, I got my own life, my own woman. Ain't got no interest in "back-tracking" —even if you *did* switch and come back to the "race".

ZENA: *(Turns to go)* Good-bye and good luck.

*(*REUBEN *grabs her hand)*

REUBEN: Diamond ring.

(Pause, she "casually" pulls her hand away. He picks some confetti out of her hair as she rears back.)

REUBEN: Satin gown... All them gals that slammed they doors on you down home...would be two-shades of "green" if they knew. *(Beat)* 'Guess you don't even remember their faces.

ZENA: *(Mocking)* They had faces?

REUBEN: *(Smiles)* Give yourself a new birth name, Zena?

ZENA: Listen, this "Auto"-thing goes on this whole week—

REUBEN: So?

ZENA: So, don't plan on lurking around, spying on me and my husband, Reuben.

REUBEN: *(Laughs)* Oh, just 'cause you living "white", I'm supposed to want to "mess with you"? Well, that's thinking like a proper white lady, all right.

ZENA: Don't make trouble!

REUBEN: What I'm gonna do? Send down to that one-mule country courthouse down in the Delta— for some faded papers with our names on it? I couldn't care less if you went up in smoke, woman. "Trouble"!? You the one who could get "me" fired.

ZENA: I would never—*never*—

(He curtly waves her off.)

REUBEN: Who you, lady? Never seen you before in my life.

(They both turn and go in opposite directions, then stop in separate pools of light; dazed.)

(Lights cross fade, as BRIAN enters with champagne. The ballroom music soars and then suddenly becomes dissonant, jangled. ZENA starts to keel over, BRIAN grabs for her.)

BRIAN: *(Calling out)* Help me, somebody! My wife!

(Lights cross fade, ETTA appears, shaking her bones, the music and crowd noise disappears. BRIAN freezes in place.)

ZENA: I'm all right! Please, I'm fine—fine!!!

(ETTA drapes ZENA in a very simple print dress over her gown.)

(Lights cross fade. The past)

(A snarling dog is heard. ETTA holds up a string of fresh caught fish and wields a knife.)

ETTA: Shut up, Lazarus! Lay down!! Down I said, down!!

ZENA: You miss Etta?

(ETTA studies ZENA.)

ETTA: So. You Zena. Little girl they call "Snow".

ZENA: *Nobody* dares call me that no more!

ETTA: Oh, she grown, now, huh? C'mon in.

ZENA: Maybe I shouldn't. Don't really believe in conjure.

ETTA: But you still wanna know what the bones say, don't ya? Um-hum. Sure you wanna know. *(Pause, holds up string of fish and knife pause)* Rest ya feet, stop propping up my door. *(Pause)* Heard y'all had bad harvest over in Bethany County.

ZENA: And I'm still nursing, too.

ETTA: Got me some fish bone soup boiled up you can take back, got fresh caught trout—

ZENA: *(Shakes head)* Obliged but I—

ETTA: *(Sharp)* Empty belly ain't nothing to be shame of! Sit!

ZENA: Look, thing is—my man's got so he can't breathe without swilling "white lightening".

ETTA: He the "guitar" man and his daddy was a gui-tar man, and I knew his daddy's daddy and he was ah gui—

ZENA: He's a fall down drunk. Not the man I married. Our Boss Man's about to throw us off the place. *(Pause)* So. You gotta charm or something I can—

ETTA: None that you'll believe in, nope. *(She calmly wields her knife, cleaning fish.)* He's a colored man feeding off dead dreams.

ZENA: Well, I got a powerful set a dreams of my own!!

ETTA: Gal, you got a bushel full, all right. And so does your other man.

ZENA: I only got me *one* somebody, and that's my husband—and that's the only one I want. What you talking 'bout?

ETTA: *(Grabbing ZENA)* I'm talking 'bout, you got maps writ all over your face! That's what I'm talking 'bout.

ZENA: *(Mocking)* You don't say? So, I'm in for travel!

ETTA: Honey, I don't know what you "in for". That's up to God and the Devil. *(She pulls off the string of bones from around her neck, throwing them to the ground, studying the pattern.)* Humph.

ZENA: *(Mocking dismissal)* Listen, my babies too weak to go anywhere. Reuben's too full of whiskey to make it down the road.

(ETTA *just stares at her pointedly)*

ETTA: You ain't lying.

ZENA: What you staring at?

(ETTA *reaches into her bosom.)*

ETTA: This here's supposed to be one of the nails from the true Cross—it come by my Great-gran by way of slavery. Here. Keep it in the pouch—you better have it.

ZENA: *(Skeptical)* How come?

ETTA: Oh, and might as well know now. There'll be another little heart pressing on your breast bone one day.

ZENA: "Wrong", midwife say I'm too torn from the birthing I just done—that's all over.

ETTA: Oh, she's just full of spit and vinegar, ain't she? Just keep in mind that all trails— *(Holding up her necklace of bones)* Sooner or later they all lead back to where they started.

ZENA: "What?" "What?"

ETTA: Take this food for the children.

ZENA: Ms Etta, I don't mean no disrespect, but I—

ETTA: *(Stops her)* Looka here, there's a white hot day, way up ahead on your path—you step careful, 'hear!? *(Pause)* Step awful, awful careful!

Scene Three

(Lights cross fade. The present. ZENA *and* BRIAN'*s hotel room. There is the sound of a T V news program coming from a place that suggests a television in the room.)*

*(*ETTA *remains in the shadows as* ZENA *unzips and removes her ball gown, stands in her slip, lets her hair down.)*

ZENA: Nonsense. Superstitious "mumbo-jumbo".

(Sound of BRIAN'*s voice calling out from the shadows.)*

BRIAN: Wendy? Darlin? *(He enters.)* You resting? Don't watch T V in the dark. Feel better?

(He turns on the lights. She is drying her hair. He has several packages in his hands. He undresses.)

ZENA: *(Pause. She watches, speaking to T V.)* Look at that crowd. Look at them throwing things at those kids. Lookit that...the kid's bleeding. Gawd.

BRIAN: What's all this? *(He glances over at the T V.)*

ZENA: The Negro kids down in Arkansas. Crowd won't let 'em—see that! Lookit their faces!

BRIAN: President Eisenhower sent in the troops, they'll handle it. Meanwhile, let's have you rest.

ZENA: *(Watching)* This is why I left the South.

BRIAN: Of course, of course. But change is difficult for most Southerners to accept. You understand that better than I do.

ZENA: *(Watching)* Aaah! He spit on that child— D'you *see* that!

(He turns off the television)

BRIAN: Didn't the nurse say to rest? *(Pause)* Sweet Saint Frances, when you keeled over like that. Jesus. *(He nuzzles her lovingly, caressing her womb.)* She could *hear* it. Imagine. She could actually, already *hear* the tiny heart...

ZENA: *(Pause)* I still don't believe it.

BRIAN: Seven years of prayers. Novenas. Rosaries. Ha. What'd I tell you? What'd I tell you, all along? That we'd have a miracle! A blessed, goddamn miracle.

ZENA: She could hear it, already hear it.

(He pulls out a teddy bear from the package. The bear wears a baby's bib and a with the logo: "Motor Capital of the World")

BRIAN: *(Laughing)* Lookit me, shameless. Can't wait to get corny, I know. "Mum and Da" —godammit, that's gonna be *us! Finally!*

(She kisses him.)

(He removes his shirt and tie, sipping scotch.)

BRIAN: *(Pause, indicates his pajamas)* Damn, this Detroit's a scorcher, huh.

ZENA: So many Negroes, too. Around. Not like the suburbs, is it.

BRIAN: "Brian Patrick Syms" —how's that sound?

ZENA: I—still can't quite *believe* it.

BRIAN: Or, is it too—you know. Look, anything *you* want, I'm for. How 'bout, "Elizabeth" if it's a— d'you like that for a girl?

ZENA: Mmm.

BRIAN: Hey. And, when they "ask"—we tell 'em they come from a long line of hardworking, God-fearing women and proud soldiers...fighters. *(Pause)* None came came from "dirt-grubbing Paddies." *(Toasts)* The mighty Syms clan. *(Pause)* Once we're home we

better start arranging for the christening. Go back to
church. Start going back to Confession...

(She holds the teddy bear.)

(A buzzer. She's startled.)

ZENA: Don't let him in!!

(BRIAN is baffled)

ZENA: Ha. Just babbling. Tee-vee upset me.

*(BRIAN moves to the shadows, muffled voices, she waits.
She waits.)*

*(He wheels on a room service tray, with a bouquet of flowers,
champagne, bowls of sherbet.)*

BRIAN: Here's for you, "Mum".

*(She claps, delighted, hugs him, they crawl into bed with the
sherbet, start feeding each other.)*

ZENA: *(Pause)* "Hungry." We'll *never* use that word in
our house.

(He kisses her)

BRIAN: "Our house." *(Kisses)* "Our house."

ZENA: Squeeze me tighter. Tighter....

(She starts kissing him fiercely)

BRIAN: Whoa—whoa, shouldn't we be more careful?

ZENA: I said, tighter!!

(As he covers her with kisses)

BRIAN: Wild lady, lovely...lovely...

(Lights cross fade to REUBEN's room in a rooming house.)

*(We hear PEARL's voice coming from the shower as she sings
a few bars of gospel music.)*

(REUBEN lies on his bed strumming his guitar.)

REUBEN: *(Singing)*
...Early in the morning, round half-past five
Rattle snake bit me but I'm still alive
I got snake bite...
I got snake bite love...
(Speaking) Don't be no fool.

(PEARL, a pretty dark-skinned woman, enters in a towel, drying off from a shower. She starts rubbing Reuben's shoulders)

PEARL: Who's a fool?

REUBEN: *(Smiling, holding his arms out wide)* Come here.

PEARL: *(Playfully shakes her head)* Too hot. Turn the record player on, I wanna hear me some Nat King Cole.

(She starts to cross over to an unseen radio, but REUBEN grabs her, pulling her down on the bed. He begins urgent love making.)

PEARL: *(Laughing)* Reu—wait... What's got into you?

(Lights go down on them)

(The sound of squalling infant comes up sharp, then subsides. Silence)

(Lights up. REUBEN and ZENA both wake with a startle, from their two separate areas on stage. They sit up. Their mates wake up beside them.)

PEARL: *(To REUBEN)* What "babies"?

REUBEN: What?

PEARL: You said "my babies..."

REUBEN: "What?" I said, "what"? When?

BRIAN: *(To ZENA)* What about our babies?

ZENA: What?

PEARL: You dreaming 'bout our kids already, huh?!

(REUBEN *leaps up, lights a cigarette.*)

PEARL: You been saying that over and over. "My babies, my babies..."

REUBEN: I never talk in my sleep.

PEARL: What they look like? Our babies to come?

REUBEN: *(Pause)* Go back to sleep.

BRIAN: *(To* ZENA*)* You were really going there... something about "babies...save my babies..."

PEARL: *(To* REUBEN, *caressing him)* Did we have a boy or a girl in your dream?

REUBEN: *(Sharp)* CUT IT OUT! *(Covering)* Sorry, honey— sorry. Hey. Let's look it up. Where the "dream book" at? *(He pulls a book from under the bed. He finds a page in the dream book.)* "Babies. Babies." Here it go— "4-5-3" — "Dream of a cradle" — "4-5-3." Tomorrow I'll put down ten bucks on "4-5-3".

PEARL: *(Hugging him)* I still say my "S & H Green Stamps" more reliable then playing these old street numbers...

BRIAN: *(Pause, singing to* ZENA*)* "You are my lucky star...."

(BRIAN *rocks* ZENA)

ZENA: What if God punishes us for wanting too much?

BRIAN: *(Gently)* And here I thought we Irish were superstitious. *(Beat)* Nobody's gonna tell me the Almighty's cruel enough to snatch away dreams, Honey.

(REUBEN *grabs his guitar starts strumming.*)

PEARL: *(Jumping up)* I forgot to say my prayers! *(She kneels down, clasping her hands.)*

REUBEN: Honey, I'm sure Jesus can excuse this one time.

PEARL: Don't make fun of my faith, Reuben.

(He kneels down beside her.)

REUBEN: I'm the one gonna be finally baptized, ain't I?
(He peeks up from his prayers, playfully. Singing)
I went to the cross roads, fell down on my bended
knee...
Cried Lord ha' mercy, Lord ha' mercy on me. *(Pause)*
See? It ain't *all* "devil music."

*(PEARL and BRIAN hug their mutual partners as ZENA
and REUBEN stare out into the shadows.)*

ZENA: *(To BRIAN)* I *deserved* to take my chance at a
better life. I'm not ashamed. It's my responsibility
to give myself a better life.

BRIAN: Sh-h-h-h-h-h. Just watch me get us everything
we need. Just watch. *(Yawning)* Better set the alarm.
(Taking one last drink) Most of those guys, tonight.
(Pause) Ivy-Leaguers with their class rings and their
country-club, "Harvard" talk. *(Downs another drink)*
Sons-of-bitches hadda go to "university" to learn how
to sell—can you beat that?

ZENA: They're nothing to you. Bugs under foot.

(BRIAN holds up a newspaper)

BRIAN: D'you catch this "Auto-rama" ad in the paper,
"Mum"? *(Notices another ad)* Hey, you! *Strangers on a
Train*'s playing just down the street.

(He hands paper to ZENA)

ZENA: *(Smiling)* You mean, it's on a double bill with
your "favorite." *(Imitating a voice)* "Shane!" "Come
back, Shane!"

BRIAN: "Come back, Shane!"

ZENA: *(Pause)* D'you see how that man spit in that
Negro girl's face?

BRIAN: Wendy, let's leave it to Mister Eisenhower, 'kay?
Now, sleep. They're children, they won't be hurt.
Nothing for you Southern Belles to worry about.

ZENA: *(Icy)* Hey!! You met a cafeteria waitress at a
Harvest Dance, there was no "Southern Belle"!

BRIAN: Just *kidding.*

ZENA: Well, don't!

(He's baffled.)

ZENA: There's nothing "gentry" about me. We've both
had our hard-tack roads. I've never seen a mint-julip or
a marble pillar in my life.

BRIAN: Who cares? Huh? Huh? All right, so I'm a night
school refuge outta Baltimore, tenement Irish. And
you—okay, you're a cafeteria waitress from—well, who
cares? Who the hell cares? We're making ourselves into
"somebodies," that's what counts in the "Land of the
Free," Wendy. *(Holding her)* Everybody—everybody in
the ballroom every night, even the so-called, high-class
snooty swells—they're all inventions, too, just like us,
don't you see that? *(He pours himself a long drink)*

(ZENA pointedly takes the drink out of BRIAN's hand.
They get into the bed.)

REUBEN: *(Singing to himself, softly)* "Lord Ha' mercy."
"Ha' mercy on me." We gonna have us one of them
wedding cakes that got three-four rows of white-
cloud icing. Mini, bride and groom..

PEARL: I got three sets of cousins coming from
Memphis.

REUBEN: *(Rubbing noses with her)* Cake or no cake,
I'm getting my "sweets", that's all I care about.

PEARL: *(Yawning)* You gonna make a great Daddy
when you finally do become one.

(REUBEN *stops cold*)

PEARL: One thing 'bout church-going men, they don't walk out on they families, like a lotta these "no counts" out here on the streets, know what I mean?

(REUBEN *rises, paces.*)

PEARL: Honey?

REUBEN: (*Pause, sharp*) Too stuffy in here! Damn fan ain't nothing but junk!

BRIAN: (*Yawning, tucking* ZENA *in*) Blessed Mary, no child of mine'll have toes sticking out of busted, hand-me-down shoes. (*He leaps up, lifts up a pair of his shoes, he also takes* ZENA's *one high heel in his hand.*) Where's your other one? Make sure ole "Uncle Jimmy" takes care of these by morning...

(ZENA *seizes the shoes.*)

ZENA: He's not your "uncle"—give me those.

BRIAN: Humm? (*He's distracted as he searches for then finds her other heel.*)

(ETTA *appears like an apparition comes from the shadows, shaking her string of necklace bones. The moan of* REUBEN's *blues harmonica is heard.*)

ZENA: (*Re the shoes*) I'll polish them myself.

(BRIAN, *bewildered, lifts the shoes out of* ZENA's *reach*)

BRIAN: Sweetheart, I know you Southerners love to take pity on the Colored—

ZENA: Brian—

BRIAN: Shining shoes is what Uncle Jimmy's down in the lobby getting paid for.

ZENA: (*Covering; smiling awkwardly*) Just give me my damn shoes.

BRIAN: *(Kissing her hands)* Now-now, pity or no pity,
I'll not have my Mrs Syms sully her lily-white—

*(ZENA "playfully" takes away her shoes, and starts twirling
BRIAN around the room, trying to distract him, and singing
a tease version of Dina Shore.)*

ZENA: *(Singing)* See the U S A
In your Cherv-rolet...

(He takes her heels back in his hand.)

BRIAN: It's not your place, m'darling.

ZENA: *(As she starts to tickle BRIAN)* Lemme at those
shoes—lemme at those shoes—

BRIAN: Bloody hell if I'll let you demean yourself like
a— *(Stops, then, shouting)* My blessed Mother scrubbed
on her hands and knees for all those high and mighty
Baltimore Protestants. Looking down their noses at her
like she was some kinda Mammy—! YOU WILL NOT
SHINE SHOES! *(Silence, then, softening)* Is this me? Is
this— *(Kissing her hands)* Please, I take it all back—
Please? Please.

PEARL: *(To REUBEN)* Jesus forgive us for "shacking up"
before holy matrimony.

REUBEN: Jesus got a lot more to forgive offa me than
this.

PEARL: In church. Sisters point me out to their little girls
and say, "Be like Sister Pearl." *(Pause)* I can't side step
the truth.

REUBEN: Nunno, you keep your eyes on what's coming
come October. The Hall, the dress, the tux, the cake,
the band—all paid for, down to every last, ever-loving
penny. *(He holds up PEARL's ring finger.)* And you gonna
have you a diamond ring, if it's the last thing I do.
(Pause) All of it paid for. Nothing on no credit. Right?
Right? Remember, that's how come we're waiting.

(PEARL *kisses* REUBEN *passionately, then pulls back.)*

PEARL: Truth is truth. I'm living "double-sided."
God knows it. I know it. *(Pause. She suddenly drops
to her knees in prayer.)*

(ZENA *and* REUBEN *stand in their respective places, staring
out into empty space—lights shift.)*

Scene Four

*(The sound of heavy downpour rain. December, 1947.
The past)*

(The sound of the squalling infants. ZENA *rises from the bed
holding an infant wrapped in a bundle of rags, the* MIDWIFE
[same actress playing ETTA, *but younger] enters, holding a
second infant, bundled in rags.)*

(REUBEN *stands in the shadows with his back to the
audience, swaying in a barely coherent, drunken state.)*

REUBEN: *(Shouting)* Lord, you wanna punish
somebody? Punish me—not them...not my babies!

MIDWIFE: Zena—these here youngins got the croup—
got the blood-spit kind of croup—it's fixing to turn to
the pneumonia...

ZENA: They won't nurse—there must be some way to
sweat the sickness out of them—

REUBEN: *(Taking a long drink)* Father-God...take me,
punish me—

MIDWIFE: *(To* REUBEN*)* Hush up! Lookit you, swilling
moonshine with your children half-way between
this world and the next! *(To* ZENA*)* I done what I can,
they need the colored clinic over in Larkin County—

ZENA: You know that don't open till Thursday!

(REUBEN *whirls around, and tries to grab one infant from the* MIDWIFE.)

REUBEN: Wrap 'em up—I'm taking 'em over to Mercy Hospital.

MIDWIFE: Now you know good'n well, no Colored are treated over at Mercy—stop acting the fool!

ZENA: Yeah, but I look white...

MIDWIFE: (*Indicating babies*) Too bad they don't.

REUBEN: God—God—God...! Fatha-God, punish me!

MIDWIFE: (*Reaches into her pockets pulls out something, hands to* ZENA) Where's that charm Ms Etta give you?

ZENA: (*Desperate*) Where—I—dunno—did I lose it!!!?

MIDWIFE: That was a nail from the true Cross...!

REUBEN: (*Indicating the babies*) Here's my "true Cross"—right here—! Here's my Cross!

ZENA: (*Yanking the baby out of* REUBEN'*s arms*) Don't be blaming "God"—where's my babies' blankets? Huh? So they can keep the cold away?

REUBEN: Zena, please...

ZENA: Ain't you the man? You promised me a brick house. With walls where the wind can't blow through on it's way to Hades—so, where is my house?

REUBEN: Zena—please, don't—not now—Zena, please—please—please!

(*Lights cross-fade back to hotel room, the present. Night*)

(ZENA *checks that* BRIAN *is sleeping. Steps forward, whispers to the air.*)

ZENA: (*Indicating her heart, pause*) And, as long as Momma never forgets you, you'll keep me safe. You'll help Momma through this trial. Yes. (*Indicating*

her womb) This one is gonna. Turn out "all right." *(Shuts
her eyes, hums a lullaby)* That's it, show Momma how to
rest easy... *(She hums a soft lullaby smiling. A moment.
Her eyes open in wide-eyed panic.)* Help me "rest"!!

(Lights shift.)

Scene Five

(Next morning)

*(*REUBEN *wakes in a startled fit, sits up in bed,* PEARL
is gone.)

REUBEN: Zena?

*(Checks to make sure she has left. He pulls out his guitar
case, reaches into a deeper compartment, takes out a small
snake-skin purse, holds it up to the spotlight.)*

(Lights cross fade.)

(The hotel restaurant. ZENA *and* BRIAN *sit at a small table
having breakfast. She's dressed in a pretty summer sun dress,
he in a summer suit and tie.)*

*(*LLOYD *sits beside them, also in summer suit.)*

*(The sound of a large crowd surrounding them fades up,
soft violins are heard.)*

(She holds up one of the pamphlets from the table.)

ZENA: I still say wives should be allowed to tour the
factories along with you men.

LLOYD: *(To* BRIAN*)* Charming. Isn't she just charming?

ZENA: If a woman's poor enough to have to *work* in
factories, then why can't women *tour* the factories along
with you fellows?

LLOYD: A mother-to-be....

*(*BRIAN *smiles,* ZENA *does a double take.)*

LLOYD: Ah, yes, I guess as much from the "fainting spell" last night. Stork's gonna pay a visit, huh? *(To ZENA)* And you still wanna walk around a grimey factory. Now, that's what I call hubby-dedication.

BRIAN: *(To ZENA)* Where we're going's no place for ladies, Beloved. There'll be half-naked men—

ZENA: *(Playful to LLOYD)* Humm—I wanna see "that"

LLOYD: HA! God almighty Bri Syms you're a lucky so-and-so with this lady.

BRIAN: *(To ZENA)* ...Men'll be working right up next to giant vats of liquid, white hot steel. Suffocating heat. Dirt. Sweat.

(PEARL enters, dressed in a waitresses uniform and carrying a platter of food, she approaches BRIAN and ZENA with a friendly smile.)

(*If necessary pancakes can be eliminated for just coffee.)

PEARL: *(Placing food on the table)* Here we go...M'am, Sirs...piping hot blue berry pancakes just sopping in maple syrup.

(ZENA offers a friendly, silent smile. LLOYD ignores PEARL, gets up, calls out.)

LLOYD: *(Calling)* Harris!! *(He kisses ZENA's hand)* Won't you excuse me for a moment, please.

(LLOYD rushes off as PEARL freshens BRIAN's coffee.)

BRIAN: Now, that's what I call Michigan hospitality—huh, Sweetheart? Thank you, Miss.

PEARL: My pleasure, Sir. My pleasure. How y'all enjoying the auto show?

BRIAN: Oh, marvelous—marvelous.

PEARL: *(Pouring his coffee)* Here, let's freshen this up for you...

BRIAN: See, m'wife and I are here from Fort Wayne, Indiana. Never set foot in the Motor Capital before. Can't wait to see those amazing car assembly plants.

PEARL: And make sure you see the "Morton Salt" plant—got pyramids of pure salt, thirty stories high.

BRIAN: Say, are you from down South? I mean the accent—my wife here's from—

ZENA: You're keeping this poor woman from her customers, darling. (*Smiles to* PEARL)

(REUBEN *enters in his janitor's uniform. He crosses down stage carrying a stack of hand-held American flags.* PEARL *gazes lovingly at him for a beat,* ZENA *tries, but cannot ignore him,* BRIAN *is oblivious.*)

PEARL: (*Nods, smiling*) Y'all enjoy De-troit, now. Welcome to the "Motor City." (*She moves off, miming taking orders from other customers.*)

BRIAN: "*Bon appetit*"— (*Taking her hand*) You're be eating for two, remember.

(ZENA *smiles silently.*)

(LLOYD *returns, pointing.*)

LLOYD: (*A sudden broad smile and wave*) Brian, take a look. (*Points*) Short, cocky fella in the yellow tie. Blake Myers from the Southern Division. He's your competition. Watch him. Study every blink. Pal around with him as much as you can. Get to know his "Achilles Heel" so to speak.

BRIAN: Absolutely.

LLOYD: Never forget, you're my boy, Boy. Let's make sure we get an Indiana man into the Regional Spot. We're counting on you.

ZENA: (*Looking*) He'll make his move, Lloyd.

LLOYD: 'Course he will, he's got you. *(He sees someone, jumps up, kissing* ZENA's *hand. Calling)* Townsend!! *(Playfully to* ZENA*)* Excuse me, You stay right there!

*(*PEARL *crosses to them a with coffee pot.)*

PEARL: More coffee, anybody?

*(*BRIAN *nods and smiles,* ZENA *shakes her head.)*

PEARL: *(To* ZENA*)* Don't mind my saying so— Sure is a pretty dress...

*(*ZENA *smiles, as* PEARL *smiles and exits.)*

BRIAN: See, what I tell you? Women admire you, honey.

ZENA: If only I could sit in some of those sales conferences, give you some pointers.

BRIAN: Hey—I only see one of us with wearing pants at this table—and—wave, honey—

(They wave, he toasts her with his coffee cup.)

BRIAN: *(Bogart voice)* "Here's looking at you, kid."

(They suddenly stop and wave)

BRIAN: Betty Sallmier told Lloyd how much she's looking forward to working with you on the Ladies Tea.

ZENA: *(Looking)* Betty Sallmier. All she talked last night was recipes. You'd think her brains were marinated.

BRIAN: Pal, that's not very nice.

ZENA: I'm *not* very nice.

*(*LLOYD *returns.)*

LLOYD: All right, folks, Chrysler's limos just pulled up, c'mon, Bri, let's get in the saddle. Don't forget, you and that Blake fellow are neck in neck—but it's up to you to snatch the "bit".

ZENA: Somebody mentioned that he raises "pure-bred" greyhounds or something or other. Tell him you're thinking of getting a dog and ask for advice.

LLOYD: *(Taking her hand)* Ha! Isn't she something!? Sure you're not a salesman?

(BRIAN kisses her good-bye, he and LLOYD exit.)

(The restaurant music continues.)

(Blues harmonica riff as REUBEN enters sweeping— ZENA opens her compact to check her makeup, see's REUBEN's reflection, turns. He doesn't notice her.)

(Just then PEARL enters from the upstage area holding up a wrapped plate in one hand, and starts to wave towards REUBEN, who is sweeping at the opposite end of the stage and does not see her.)

(ZENA calls out to REUBEN, PEARL freezes in place as she sees this.)

ZENA: *(Calling out to REUBEN, loudly)* Excuse me, Sir!?

(REUBEN turns, sees it's ZENA, turns away continues to sweep.)

ZENA: *(Smiling broadly and gesticulating)* Sir!!?? Wonder if you could help me? *(Loudly to REUBEN, holds out a note)* Sir? Could please tell me the directions to this?

(REUBEN glares at Zena, approaches as a "servant" must. He snatches her note, reads it.)

(PEARL watches. REUBEN glances around to make sure no one is watching. PEARL momentarily ducks into the shadows.)

ZENA: *(Calling out, waving)* Hi, Margie! See you at the tea. Tell Betty I'm on my way to the meeting.

(The shadow passes, she and REUBEN look around cautiously. He takes a pencil from his pocket, writes on her note.)

REUBEN: Here. You're looking for Belle Isle Park.
Straight down Jefferson Avenue.

ZENA: *(Quiet and tense)* Fine. Noon.

(ZENA exits.)

*(REUBEN exits in the opposite direction. Upstage,
PEARL watches.)*

(Lights cross fade.)

Scene Six

(The basement)

*(REUBEN slides in a small platform. Two seats and a minimal
steering wheel represent the inside body of a brand new car.
He slaps rags against the steering wheel of the car, back and
forth and back and forth with more and more force and more
and more force...and singing over and over to himself:)*

REUBEN: Sun gonna shine in my back door someday.
Gonna SHINE IN MY BACK...
Bitch.

*(Enter PEARL, she sneaks up and places her hands on his
eyes, he jumps a bit, recovers.)*

PEARL: Surprise!

REUBEN: Hey-hey-hey-here's my "lollipop."

(He takes her on his lap)

PEARL: Guess what? The kids in Little Rock got into the
school!

(They both slap hands, laughing)

PEARL: "Lunch time." *(Offers cake she has wrapped in a
bag)* Cook upstairs made so many batches-he's begging
us all to take extra.

(He gobbles down the cake.)

REUBEN: You gonna spoil my appetite.

PEARL: Depends on how strong of an "appetite" you got, baby.

REUBEN: *(Smiling)* Behave yourself now.

PEARL: *(Smiles)* Long as you do, I will.

REUBEN: *(Smiles)* Uh-oh!!

PEARL: *(Playfully frustrated)* "Reuben"! *(Then holding up the plate)* Why you eat around the chocolate frosting like that? Thought you liked icing.

(He nibbles at her neck.)

REUBEN: Lemme gobble up some a this here!!

(Swatting him, playfully)

PEARL: Quit, fool.

(He points.)

REUBEN: Which one of these you want?

PEARL: The mint green Chevy, that's what I want.

REUBEN: But we'd knock 'em dead in this maroon Thunderbird. Get in.

PEARL: But if they catch us.

REUBEN: Jamison's at lunch. *(Pulls her into the car)* Let's christen it 'fore the whites get to it when it's hauled upstairs.

(They kiss long and hard.)

REUBEN: Let's test "drive".

PEARL: In the basement?

REUBEN: Pretend. Dream. Make believe. Va-rrr-oom!! Put your head back. We headed over to Canada...yeah, head on out to open fields with prancing horses, and

farms planted in high corn combing the air...and
woods, thicker—thicker.

(A blues riff is heard in REUBEN's *head. Then* ZENA's *voice)*

ZENA: Reu!! You drive too fast!

(He stops.)

PEARL: Thank goodness no children of ours'll be
born down South. Huh?

(He swings out of the car, paces.)

REUBEN: I want us to have a *brick* house, you
understand? A brick house. And guess what?
Ain't gonna be no more of me cleaning toilets,
sweeping up "kotex..."

PEARL: But the factories make you sick.

(He holds out newspaper)

PEARL: *(Reading)* Ha!! Thank you, All Mighty God!

REUBEN: Thank you, "N A A C P.". Bus company *gotta*
hire us.

PEARL: There's a test.

REUBEN: Hell, drove a tractor from age eleven, mule
'fore that. Driving I do. Yeah. Shit, yeah.

*(*PEARL *gives him a look, he laughs)*

REUBEN: I know, I know—I'm "saved."

(He begins dancing PEARL *around.)*

REUBEN: *(Singing)* Gonna get up in the morning
Believe I'll dust my broom.
Gonna get up in the morning
Believe I'll dust my broom...
Want me a good woman
To help me dust my broom...

PEARL: Sweet, there's a crumb on your lip. *(She brushes his mouth with her hand.)* Got it. *(Pause)* Who was that gal in the sundress that was all up in your face.

REUBEN: *(Polishing, not looking up)* What gal?

PEARL: *(Pause)* That "Saltine" leaning over you in the lobby. What that Cracker want?

REUBEN: *(Polishing)* Oh, you mean the one who come give me a million bucks?

(PEARL gives him a "look".)

REUBEN: Honey, some of 'em just ask me for directions, y'know.

PEARL: Humph! In a pig's eye! Wanted a piece of "tail"—that's what. And lingering all over you and carrying on!

REUBEN: Baby, don't pay 'em no mind. Ain't worth it.

(She points to where he is polishing.)

PEARL: You missed a spot. *(Pause)* All of 'em upstairs there: "glittering" and sashaying and flinging they pointed titties at everything that's got two legs, and a "ding-a-ling" in-between. *(Pause)* Rest assured, there's always a few of 'em after some Colored "you-know-what."

REUBEN: Why fuss about crackers we'll never see again in life.

(PEARL grabs the rag from REUBEN, begins polishing)

PEARL: You still ain't got this spot, right, Sweetheart. Do like this, see here...? *(Polishing)* And them so-called "upstanding" cracker husbands upstairs in they silk shirts and ties, ha! Tell me how many of 'em sneak off to "nigga town" for some "poon-tang" soon as the sun go down!

(REUBEN takes the rag from her.)

REUBEN: Titus told me the Masonic Lodge give him and Dolora a cut rate on they wedding. Let's check it out.

PEARL: "Auto-rama" my foot! What I wanna know is how many of 'em upstairs there are walking 'round with some of "us" in they blood! Tell me that!

(REUBEN slaps his rag hard against the "car" as she watches him.)

REUBEN: Excuse me, ma'am—you seen Pearl Henderson 'round here? Can I please speak to her?

PEARL: *(Checking REUBEN's polish)* Good. It's spotless. *(Pause)* Something 'bout that gal—one called you over? See, I served her and her "Ofay" husband— Oh, she do the "Ms Anne" stuff, but—mmm—something "Lili-fied" 'bout her, I swear.

REUBEN: You and Thelma going shopping? Pick me up some razors, will ya?

PEARL: She got some kinda nigga blood in her, how much you wanna bet? I got radar can always spot it.

(REUBEN slaps his rag against the chaise for final polish)

REUBEN: Oh, you a Conjure Woman, now?

PEARL: I tell you she's a bonafide brown "lily" passing— something swept cross me when I poured her coffee, looking into her eyes. Just didn't pay it no mind at the time!

(REUBEN concentrates on folding up the rags.)

REUBEN: Well, if she "is" one, it's her business. How many of the rest of us would try it if we had a chance.

PEARL: Reu!

REUBEN: Hell, everything you want without "stop signs" thrown up in your face... If they could, most of these "Spooks" out here would be right up there with her.

PEARL: Reuben! Ain't you proud of your Color, and the Colored race?

REUBEN: Can't philosophize and work at the same time, Pearlie.

PEARL: I do hope I'm marrying me a proud race man.

REUBEN: I'm proud—what I gotta do? Advertise it? Honey, Thelma 'en them gonna leave you behind, if you don't catch up.

PEARL: And the heifer was justa "Miss Ann-ing" me when I took they order.

(They mime opening doors, and cross into another area of light. The sound of traffic comes up sharp. Sound of cars. They are in the street.)

(REUBEN calls and waves off-stage to an unseen woman.)

REUBEN: Thelma! Wait up for Pearl!

PEARL: Maybe I won't do my shopping—have lunch with you.

(She studies his face.)

REUBEN: C'mon, then. *(Pause)* But when Thelma come flauntin' some fancy threads that she got on sale, don't come crying to me.

PEARL: *(Pause, then)* Where you headed, Baby?

REUBEN: Same ole same... Bo-Bo got a crap game going on the roof.

(An unseen black women's voice calls out)

WOMAN'S VOICE: Pearl? You coming or what?

(PEARL studies REUBEN for a long beat, then turns to exit in the direction of the voice)

PEARL: *(Blowing him a kiss)* Stay Sweet.

(REUBEN watches her go, waves. A beat. Lights cross fade)

Scene Seven

(The park—that afternoon)

(Gulls are heard and the lapping river current. REUBEN *and* ZENA *enter. Sunlight glints across their faces.)*

(A silence as they stare at each other.)

REUBEN: This the back end of the park. Used mostly by Colored.

ZENA: So?

REUBEN: So, ain't likely none of y'fancy cracker tourist friends'll happen by this way.

ZENA: Oh, you're a fine one for contempt.

REUBEN: Look, I'm *came!* Now, what the hell is this about!? Oh, yeah...wait...

*(*REUBEN *opens up his lunch pail, takes out a rather tattered, but once fancy snakeskin purse, he opens it, pulling out a rough-hewn crucifix tied to a long string. There is also a small furry tail attached to the cross. He offers both to* ZENA, *who doesn't take them)*

ZENA: "What?"

REUBEN: Bertha wanted you to have this.

ZENA: *(Staring at the bag)* Jesus.

(An unseen voice calls out as if in ZENA's *mind. It is* BERTHA-MAE.)*

BERTHA-MAE: *(Calling out)* JESUS!!

REUBEN: Promised her on her deathbed that if we ever crossed path...I'd.

ZENA: I hope she's in the hottest deepest drop of Hell with the flames licking her face.

(REUBEN *holds out the objects but* ZENA *doesn't take them.*)

(*Lights cross fade and Conjure woman enters from the shadows, her back to the audience, speaking in the voice of* BERTHA-MAE *and wielding a large pair of scissors at* ZENA.)

BERTHA-MAE: Pray with me—"Snow". You may be the color of grits, but you ain't pure like Jesus. You a nigga. Your yella Momma rutted with half the midnight rednecks of Eden County. Yep. But when the white men come after *your* little "cherry" you gonna think twice, before you disgrace *me*! Oh, yes!

(*Lights change back to present*)

REUBEN: Zena!?

ZENA: (*Pointing to the calico bag*) Man, are you loco? Holding on to this since—?

BERTHA-MAE: (*Calling out to the air*) You already had one whippin, want another one? First we gotta cut off all this straight white-folks hair—you too prideful... C'mon, "Snow." Stop flinching. More hurt go into it, the more sin guaranteed to come out. Darlin, the devil's gonna burn it all off anyway when you get to hell. God, why didn't a send her nigger hair? Kneel down. C'mon. I'm gonna save you from turning out like your momma if it's the last thing I do, this side of the Judgment. (*She turns and gestures towards* ZENA.) Save her, Jesus.

(ZENA *flings the bag into the water,* REUBEN *immediately reaches to retrieve it.*)

REUBEN: Never throw out the cross.

ZENA: (*Shaking her head*) Still a country hick full of superstitions.

REUBEN: Oh, you a real, live, sophisticated "white" lady, now, huh? Chopping cotton and taking your butt to outhouses never happened.

ZENA: *(Firm)* You better leave that laying right where it is.

(He drops the bag to the ground)

REUBEN: She died a real hard death.

ZENA: Good.

REUBEN: Typhus. Swept through the shacks that Spring.

ZENA: Crazy bitch wasn't even my real blood, and certainly no kinda of mother. *(Fuming)* All the so-called good folks of the County leaving such a demented—with a helpless orphan, and nobody stood up to her for me—nobody—

REUBEN: I did.

(ZENA stops. They stare)

ZENA: What about my note?

(PEARL has entered upstage in a pool of light. Lights create the impression of her watching ZENA and REUBEN from a distance. She cannot hear them, they can't see her.)

PEARL: *(As she watches)* My-my-my-my. Jesus? He's telling her: "look, I'm taken, bitch. I ain't inter-rested." He's telling her, I got me my one good woman, period—ain't he, Lord? Ain't he. *(Hums gospel as she watches them, hurt)*

ZENA: *Will* you go half and half on these gravestones for the girls, or not?

REUBEN: They *have* a granite grave stone! Maybe it's hard for you to believe—but when you cut out—I. *(Pause)* Finally saw the "bottom" of the bottom.

ZENA: Just tell me "yes" or—

REUBEN: I hired myself out double-shift to the Bellamy Plantation, and paid for a plain granite cross for the twins.

PEARL: *(To herself)* This just a test of my faith in him, ain't it, Lord? Calm down, girl. Calm down.

ZENA: But, no Colored babies in that whole town have marble. Finally, we can give them marble angels.

(ZENA hands him the bundle of cash.)

REUBEN: You handing me a white man's money to fix my dead children's graves?

ZENA: I EARNED THIS MYSELF.

REUBEN: *(Seething, pitching stones into the river)* Yeah, I'm *sure* you did.

ZENA: WHERE'S YOUR RIGHT TO LOOK DOWN ON ME?!

REUBEN: You cut out 'fore they was even laid to rest!

ZENA: Five years I put up with you day in and day out—

REUBEN: I know damn well what I was.

ZENA: You was too piss-drunk to "know." So plowed under, your vomit was your main meal.

REUBEN: Go on back down there to the Colored cemetery yaself! Naw, you don't dare—do ya!?
(He turns to go.)

ZENA: Even the last night they drew breath. You were swimming in that bottle.

(He stops, stung. PEARL continues to watch, unable to hear.)

PEARL: *(Softly to the air)* Relax, girl. Even Christ himself was tempted. "Get thee behind me, Satan."

REUBEN: Tell you what kinda fool I was. Oh, I figured you'd most likely be settled with somebody else if I came up on you again. But it never come to me I'd run into you "white".

ZENA: Why did I think you'd want to do anything
decent? Should know better.

(She turns to go. REUBEN *grabs* ZENA's *wrist.)*

REUBEN: You tell him you had brown babies come out
of you? Huh?

ZENA: You better take your hands off me.

REUBEN: My stinky nigger hands? What's it say 'bout
them for you to turn on they color?

ZENA: *(Pulling against him)* Who kept vigil all night
long, every night? I did. Where were you? Who walked
the floor with their fever screaming, huh? You?! Was it
you????!!

(A white POLICEMAN, *played by actor playing* LLOYD,
approaches out on his beat.)

POLICEMAN: *(To* ZENA*)* You okay, Miss?

*(*REUBEN *and* ZENA *whirl around to face him, he lets go of
her)*

ZENA: *(Taking* REUBEN's *arm)* Ah, yes Sir.

PEARL: *(Looking on)* Am I the one being punished
by you, God?

ZENA: *(Continuing to* POLICEMAN*)* It's—he's—.
Thank you, Officer. Everything's. Fine.

*(*POLICEMAN *takes them both in for a long beat, then curtly
moves on a short distance, still in sight.* ZENA *drops*
REUBEN's *arm.)*

ZENA: Just like old times.

REUBEN: 'Cept we useta laugh about it back when—we
started out.

ZENA: Didn't laugh that time in Rileyville.

REUBEN: Well, Rileyville was—"Rileyville".

ZENA: That scar still. Show?

REUBEN: Oh, Zee, girl. Zena.

PEARL: *(Hurt as she watches them)* Grannie Wade was right: men are hounds always sniffing for "bones," even when they gotta good meal back home.

ZENA: *(To REUBEN; as she shakes her head towards the POLICEMAN)* He's still watching, look.

(ZENA nods in the direction of the POLICEMAN, REUBEN stiffens)

(POLICEMAN remains in the shadows, staring at them.)

ZENA: He's just trying to figure it out. Is she a white woman sullying herself? Could she be one of them special niggers?

REUBEN: Don't.

ZENA: *(Pause, smiling)* "Don't"? How can I help it? *(Pause)* That rope swing you hung from that big ole sycamore so it would dangle over the creek out back.

REUBEN: Umm.

ZENA: *(Holds out her arm as he looks on)* Remember how I use to swing out on it back and forth and back and forth... cross both sides of the creek?

REUBEN: Back and forth...

ZENA: I'd get on and hold tight. Tight. Then swing out. *(Pause)* See what side of the bank the rope would carry me to, would land on. *(Pause)* And all my life, that rope's been other people's looks, glances.

PEARL: *(To herself)* Pearl, pick up your feet and go down there. *(She remains stock still)*

ZENA: ...Eyes wondering "what side the creek she belong on?" I'm on the rope dangling. Just dangling.

REUBEN: *(Silence, then)* Honey, let's have marble. But I'm gonna see to it myself, somehow. Least I can do. Zee? *(Pause)* Till the day I draw my last breath, it's my shame. Didn't even have decent blankets to wrap 'em in to send to Jesus.

ZENA: *(Soft)* We were just poor, that's all. And all the rules made sure we stayed stuck. *(Pause)* D'you ever learn how to breathe under water when you swim?

REUBEN: *(Smiles)* Wha? Nope. *(Pause)* 'Member all them fire flies? Like gold dust floating through the dark.

ZENA: *(Pause)* Rue, I just couldn't bear to see my little girls be layed in ground.

REUBEN: Don't—trouble over it no more, Baby.

ZENA: Think we woulda ever been able to tell 'em apart? You woulda spoiled 'em.

REUBEN: You bet. *(Pause)* We better quit.

(ZENA opens her purse, takes the ivory box, then the locket, opens it, holds up two small cuttings of baby hair.)

REUBEN: My babies' hair. Still just as soft as it was—

ZENA: *(Offering one of the ribbons to REUBEN)* Always carry 'em when I go traveling—can't help it, I just do. *(Pause)* You should have one.

(REUBEN delicately takes one of the ribbons, takes out his own pocket handkerchief, and places it inside, wrapping it gently and placing it inside his shirt pocket.)

REUBEN: If only...

ZENA: Sh-h-h-h-h...don't. *(A silence)* Gotta go.

(ZENA brusquely returns her piece of baby hair to the locket, the locket into the ivory box, and the box into her pouch.)

(She and REUBEN stare at each other for a beat, not knowing what else to say.)

REUBEN: So long.

ZENA: You have no idea. How overjoyed. Relieved.
I was when my Little Zena Jean, and Magdalene
Marie—those sweet faces turned out cinnamon brown.

REUBEN: Oh, yes I do.

ZENA: Oh, no you don't.

(They smile to each other as ZENA *puts on her sunglasses,
walks away.* REUBEN *does not look after her, a few beats,
he picks the snake-skin pouch from off the ground, considers,
then tosses it back down, and exits in the opposite direction.)*

*(*PEARL *enters and approaches the spot where they stood.
She picks up the snake-skin pouch, opens it and looks inside,
pulls out the squirrel tail and the crucifix. A beat. Fade out*

END OF ACT ONE

ACT TWO

Scene One

(Afternoon and evening of same day)

(Lights up on three separate areas of the stage—a tableau.)

(ZENA standing on a street corner, fanning herself.)

(BRIAN and LLOYD at the factory, stand looking out at the audience, briefcases in hand.)

(ZENA opens her pouch, pulls out the locket, a folded newspaper in her hand, appears to be searching for an address.)

(BRIAN and LLOYD stand underneath a sign reading: "FORD WELCOMES AUTORAMA TOUR OF '57")

(Tableau freezes, then: ZENA faces the audience. She fans herself, showing her newspaper.)

(The sounds of the factory up clanging, discordant. Silhouettes of figures on the assembly line, shadow BRIAN and LLOYD's faces.)

(ZENA faces SISTER NICODEMOS. She is dressed in th tight "pedal-pusher" pants of the late fifties, her hair in a stylish bun. She wears flip flop heels, dangling earrings, is apparently a heavy smoker, and chews gum which she pops and cracks through her teeth now and then, she fans herself with a hand-held fan.)

SISTER NICODEMOS: Welcome to Sistah Nicodemos...

(Sound of a screeching parakeet is heard.)

(LLOYD steps forward, gestures, mimes closing a large picture window, the factory sound is then muffled.)

LLOYD: Welcome to what we call the "Eagles Nest". Great view from this vantage point, eh?

(BRIAN looks out over the audience)

(SISTER NICODEMOS calls out to the screeching parakeet on her side of the stage.)

SISTER NICODEMOS: *(She calls out)* Shut Up, "Sheba!!" *(Then to ZENA)* And you are?

ZENA: *(Pauses)* Mrs. Mrs. Reuben Sinclair.

(SISTER NICODEMOS holds out her hand, they shake.)

SISTER NICODEMOS: How-do. Miz Sinclair.

(BRIAN looks out over the audience)

BRIAN: It's like looking down on the insides of a giant clock...

LLOYD: Assembly line—marvel of the modern age.

BRIAN: Grand. As my folks in the old country would say. Just "grand."

LLOYD: You bet your sweet ass. Feel that heat coming up off the floor?

SISTER NICODEMOS: C'mon in, just slam the screen behind ya.

(We hear an amplified slam.)

SISTER NICODEMOS: Ain't it hot—furnace hot?

ZENA: Back home we'd call this a "noon day sun".

SISTER NICODEMOS: Just sit any where, Suga. Now, that accent, you only got a trace of it—

ZENA: Mississippi originally, Laurel, Mississippi. But I been living here in De-troit so—y'know—so long.

SISTER NICODEMOS: Mississippi! Whew! I hear our people back down South, some still don't got no T Vs or inside toilets, still pump they water out the ground.

ZENA: My husband says, "outhouse or in-house, it's all still the same *stuff*."

(SISTER NICODEMOS throws her head back and cackles.)

SISTER NICODEMOS: Ha. A-men!

LLOYD: Michigan, U S A—we *know* how to put a car together. Europe only spits out "bugs" and "pea pods" and- and

BRIAN: ...And then puts wheels on 'em. They need Uncle Sam.

LLOYD: *(Toasting BRIAN)* That's the attitude!! That's precisely why you're my champion, boy.

BRIAN: *(Gesturing towards factory sound)* Mister Davis,—

(LLOYD holds up a finger.)

LLOYD: Eh?

BRIAN: "Lloyd"—this industry is my chance to make a difference, in my own, well—humble—way, in people's lives. Maybe that's a tad sentimental—

LLOYD: Nunno. You've got heart. You've got grit. You're "me" thirty years ago.

(They toast. They drink.)

(SISTER NICODEMOS studies ZENA.)

SISTER NICODEMOS: *(Pause)* Got a man in the plant?

ZENA: *(Nods)* Chryslers. He's on the day shift.

(The parakeet screeches)

SISTER NICODEMOS: Sheba! Didn't I tell you to *shut up*! Lemme cover that bird...

(SISTER NICODEMOS *exits off, briefly*, ZENA *attempts to look around but* SISTER NICODEMOS *returns.*)

SISTER NICODEMOS: Child, rest ya feet, go on, sit. So. And you been in De-troit, you say, how long?

ZENA: Well, I didn't—but it's seven years.

SISTER NICODEMOS: So. You scouting.

ZENA: Pardon me?

SISTER NICODEMOS: Scouting. Out looking for Sistahs with "the gift."

ZENA: Ha. Well, I suppose I am.

SISTER NICODEMOS: Them some pretty nails you got.

ZENA: Sweet of you to say.

(SISTER NICODEMOS *begins to study* ZENA'*s palm*, ZENA *gingerly pulls her hand back.*)

(BRIAN *and* LLOYD *continue to drink.*)

BRIAN: So. Me and Myers got a good look at each other.

LLOYD: Nothing like a good cockfight.

BRIAN: He's mighty nervous. His hands. He's constantly opening and closing his hands.

LLOYD: Student of human nature—that's it, Son. Yep, I've chosen the right man. Say, where'd you meet that one-in-a-million gal of yours?

BRIAN: Was being recruited by Cleary Inc. down in Atlanta. Back in '52. Her folks are those "ruined gentry types".

LLOYD: Sort of *Gone With the Wind* in real life.

BRIAN: She doesn't like to speak about it.

LLOYD: Understandable. Ah, if only my dearest Madeline could have known your Mrs. I always say it's the woman who civilizes the man.

BRIAN: Ha. I was certainly a "shaggy dog" until she refined me.

SISTER NICODEMOS: So. *(To* ZENA*)* How'd you find me.

ZENA: *(Holds up her newspaper) The Chronicle*—classified.

SISTER NICODEMOS: *(Re the paper)* That there's the oldest Negro newspaper in the country.

ZENA: You don't say?

SISTER NICODEMOS: First time ever consulting a spiritualist?

(Pause. SISTER NICODEMOS *whips the cloth off of a table figure, it is a medium-sized black saint, she lights a candle.)*

SISTER NICODEMOS: I don't use no bones or nothing, got my own way.

ZENA: Surprised to see so many of you Sisters listed in paper.

SISTER NICODEMOS: Why, sure. You can't just scoop out what's been bred in the bone, honey. And the old ways done been bred in us, Jesus not-withstanding, praise the Lord. Can't just peel off what we been taught, brought up to believe, now can't we?

ZENA: I wonder.

SISTER NICODEMOS: Lemme see the whites of ya eyes.

LLOYD: *(To* BRIAN*)* Usually those blue-blood types hate to marry "out of the fold" —don't they?

BRIAN: Love conquers all.

(They toast.)

LLOYD: And in seven months comes your family to support. Hopefully at *double* the salary.

BRIAN: Just let me in the bullpen.

LLOYD: The Company's pleased that you're finally having a family. Don't let her tag the boy with nothing "frilly" like "Lynford" or "Wilfred" or "Ashley" —Southerners tend to fall for that.

(Pause)

BRIAN: Right. What's your own son like? Never hear you mention him much.

LLOYD: Less said on that subject the better. *(Pause)* So, how's it feel to be up here in the "Eagles Nest" looking down on creation?

BRIAN: I'm ready to get used to it. Ha. Of course, my Rival's also ready to get used to it.

(ZENA suddenly rises to leave.)

ZENA: Y'know, on second thought, I better—

SISTER NICODEMOS: Your choice, there's the door.

(ZENA stands stock still)

ZENA: Don't mean to insult you, but—well, *(Shakes her head)* Guess, I've out grown "hoo-doo" stuff

SISTER NICODEMOS: Hoo-doo? You ain't down South no more, honey. Sister Nicodemous is a certified, genuine Spiritualist. A session is ten dollars, and by the way, I do a great wash and press for another thirteen. *(She circles ZENA, studies her hair.)* 'Course, you don't gotta press yours, like most colored women do, do ya? Got white folks hair.

ZENA: I love my hair.

SISTER NICODEMOS: *(Pause)* Ain't it the truth.

LLOYD: Up here's where we get a chance to keep an eye on the little people. *(Pointing towards the muffled noise)* Ford had the vision. *(Pause)* Niggers, Mexican wetbacks, Jew boys, probably some gypsies, all working together, all working alongside the regular men—Ford knew this would be the glory, the great thing about industry, commerce, progress.... By the way, my Granddad shook hands with Ford, once.

BRIAN: *(Pause)* Mr. Davis, shouldn't we catch up with the tour?

LLOYD: Relax, boy. Take it easy. Watch the "worker bees" down below. Tens of millions of sonofabitches would give *anything* to be up here.

(ZENA holds out her hand, SISTER NICODEMOS takes it.)

ZENA: Thank you for your time, sorry to bother you.

(SISTER NICODEMOS fans herself steadily.)

SISTER NICODEMOS: How long you been living white? *(Pause)* ...Yeah, I know, you "don't got no idea what I'm talking 'bout". And if *you* got a man in the factories, *I'm* Queen Cleopatra.

(The women study each other. Silence. Then ZENA breaks out into a laugh, with SISTER NICODEMOS joining her.)

ZENA: It's not like I'm doing something criminal.

SISTER NICODEMOS: Then stop acting like it is. *(Pause)* Sit on down here, girl.

ZENA: Who says I have to "belong" to one set of people or the other. In particular. I don't.

SISTER NICODEMOS: There's no law in nature that I know of.

(The women study each other)

ZENA: *(Pause)* A-men. *(Pause)* Anybody who's ever been caught in a rock throwing crowd of Sunday-school

knotty-heads screaming: "yellow salt-cracker-bastard"
—well, let *them* point a finger at me, but *nobody* else!
Nobody else! Dammit, all. Nobody.

BRIAN: *(To* LLOYD*)* You won't regret taking this chance
on me.

LLOYD: Don't intend to. *(Beat)* Had a recent going over
of your files.

BRIAN: *(Pause)* My quotas are wide open for anybody to
see.

LLOYD: Your quotas are "legend". You're our Indiana
legend. This is just for clarification, you see.

BRIAN: Let's have it.

LLOYD: "Religion." It's not filled in on the form.

BRIAN: Must be an oversight.

LLOYD: That's what I told the "team", of course. You
see, now that you're on the rise, it's these "details"
—that go a long way to "completing the picture".

BRIAN: I'm Presbyterian.

LLOYD: *(Pause)* That's a relief.

(They smoke, pause.)

*(*ZENA *stands again)*

ZENA: Excuse me. Pardon me.

SISTER NICODEMOS: Child, you got a match to your
butt? Then sit on back down. *(She leans in on* ZENA.*)*
What's it feel like?

ZENA: What?

SISTER NICODEMOS: To be able to be taken for, y'know,
just anybody. Go wherever you got a mind to go—
do whatever you set your heart to.

ZENA: It's. *(Pause)* Not quite what I dreamed. And not quite, "not".

SISTER NICODEMOS: Now, ain't that the truth? Ain't that always the case with dreams?

*(*BRIAN *and* LLOYD *smoke, pause.)*

BRIAN: Since we're alone here, Lloyd—well—well—

LLOYD: Spit it out.

BRIAN: The '58 pick up trucks. Rumor has it there a design flaw in the break system. *(Stops himself)* Could that be. Correct?

ZENA: *(Pause, to* SISTER NICODEMOS*)* Look, how much of the future can you tell?

SISTER NICODEMOS: How much of the future you wanna know?

LLOYD: A rumor is neither correct, nor incorrect. You just said yourself: "love conquers all".

(Pause)

BRIAN: Is there. A flaw.

LLOYD: Depends on how you define "flaw". Doesn't it.

ZENA: The thing is—

SISTER NICODEMOS: The "thing" is, "he or she" better be painted right, that's what the "thing" is.

ZENA: Fool midwife back home swore I'd never be able to—

SISTER NICODEMOS: Conceive?

BRIAN: Are there memos.

LLOYD: Have you *seen* any memos?

BRIAN: Rumor has it there are these "Inter-office Files" making the rounds in upper management. Is that true?

LLOYD: You're supposed to be "nose to nose" with your rival—find out if he's heard anything, seen anything, knows anything that you should know. If you get a "whiff" of any "secret sessions" going on anywhere, you be sure and clue me in on it.

(SISTER NICODEMOS *studies* ZENA.)

SISTER NICODEMOS: *(Pause)* And, supposed "he or she" *do* come out "carrying coal"? Suppose I can tell that. Are prepared to do what's...necessary?

ZENA: What'd you talking about?

SISTER NICODEMOS: Don't waste my time. You know what I mean.

BRIAN: *(To* LLOYD) The Company would of course recall the product.

(*A tremendous clanging sound, screams—the men look out,* BRIAN *presses against the apron of the stage as if it were a window.*)

BRIAN: What happened? That guy's hurt down there!! They need an ambulance!

(LLOYD *doesn't budge.*)

LLOYD: *(Pause)* The shop stewards'll take care of it.

(ZENA *starts to speak,* SISTER NICODEMOS *cuts her off, looking into* ZENA's *eyes. She takes a shallow transparent, glass bowl, pours some oil.*)

SISTER NICODEMOS: I don't use "bones" like the old folks did. *(She holds up the glass bowl. She lights the glass bowl a small flame leaps up. She sprinkles in a handful of flour which douses the flame. She holds the bowl up to the lamp light.)* You already got two precious hearts pressing on your soul as it is.

ZENA: My little girls! *(She crosses to the bowl, startled.)*

(LLOYD reaches into his suit pocket, pulls out a card, offers it to BRIAN.)

LLOYD: Here. This'll get your little lady's eyes to sparkling...

BRIAN: The Country Club.

LLOYD: *(Shaking his hand)* Your pretty Mrs'll be so pleased.

BRIAN: *(Pause)* Will there be a product recall on the "'58s"?

LLOYD: D'you think your Rival is asking?

(SISTER NICODEMOS holds up the flaming bowl)

(LLOYD offers BRIAN his hand.)

SISTER NICODEMOS: *(To ZENA)* Close your eyes. Whose name is the Saint gonna call? Whose name? Who?

LLOYD: Welcome to the Club. *(Lights cross fade)*

Scene Two

(REUBEN's room in the rooming house.)

(Spotlight on REUBEN, singing, he holds out the open handkerchief with baby hair.)

REUBEN: *(Singing)*
Hush, little pretty girls, don't say a word
Daddy's gonna buy you a mockingbird...

(He hears a tiny sound. It is rain, then the thin squall of a hungry infant.)

(He stuffs the wrapped handkerchief inside his shirt, then strums his guitar.)

REUBEN: How can Daddy ever have new little girls when he got y'all? *(Pause)* Send me a sign. Send me a dream. A sign. A dream.

(He falls asleep. Cross-fading lights indicate the passage of hours)

(Lights Up full. REUBEN'*s room.* PEARL *stands in a tight fitting red evening dress,* REUBEN *is stirring out of sleep, she is covering his eyes.)*

PEARL: Surprise!

REUBEN: What time is it?

PEARL: Six-thirty. Don't look yet—

REUBEN: How was work? Let's get takeout and go to the river. Too hot to be inside. We'll go blink at the moon and watch the fire flies dancing.

(She uncovers his eyes, he sees the dress: tight-fitting and flattering PEARL'*s voluptuous figure.)*

REUBEN: *(Clapping with admiration; grabbing and holding her)* Uh-oh, watch out! You gonna get my "mojo" worked up all night long—looking like that....

PEARL: *(Caressing him)* All night long—promise?

(They both giggle.)

PEARL: Took it out of "lay away". I know we don't want debt, but...

REUBEN: Baby, it is super-supreme...
(Pause, improvising a blues rift, singing)
Don't want me no Downtown woman
Got me! My baby here on my knee...
Don't want me no Downtown woman
Got me! My baby here on my knee...

PEARL: A-men.

REUBEN: My Pearlie's finer than rubies—better even then a hard-rock diamond any day.

PEARL: Only diamonds I done seen are white. *(Pause)* Only pearls come in my shade of jewel.

(He grabs a towel)

REUBEN: Ain't it the truth. Lemme run in the shower right quick.

PEARL: What'd you do for lunch—this afternoon?

REUBEN: Same ole same. You get them razor's, Babe?

(PEARL removes the dress and stands in her slip.)

PEARL: I'm *your* woman...your dark-skinned woman....

REUBEN: Only woman I got.

PEARL: "Got" and "want" is two different things. *(She holds the red dress up. Studying herself in "mirror")* Lotta Negroes'll say that red makes me look too dark.

REUBEN: *(Overlapping)* There's stupid people everywhere, Honey.

PEARL: Run into Titus in the Laundry, he say you weren't at the crap game at lunch.

REUBEN: Naw. Today I just walked the river like the country boy I am. *(Smiles)* What's this some kinda "report" I gotta turn in, or something? *(Pause)* Want "carbon copies"?

PEARL: Stop, silly. Can't I just be inter-rested in you?

(PEARL pours lather in her palm, then pats REUBEN's face. He sits draped in a towel, she begins to shave him.)

REUBEN: I can do this.

PEARL: *(Playful)* Nunno, you with a "daughter of a barber" —y'know I love to. *(As she shaves REUBEN)* Used to watch Daddy so careful—

REUBEN: I get a smooth one every time with you, Baby.

PEARL: That's right... *(Shaving REUBEN)* 'Course Daddy'd talk ya ear off if it was him. Standing here. *(Imitating father)* "Man never marry no 'blackie'. 'Cause

a too dark gal draws to much attention. A too dark gal
makes other folks sorry for a Colored man." And all the
other guys in the shop be hooting and hollering: "That's
right man, a too dark, tar-black gal so ugly, scare the
devil hisself."

REUBEN: *(Interrupting, stopping her)* Pearlie.

PEARL: *(Imitating Daddy)* "The kids off a too dark gal'd
be like pickannnies made of coal."

REUBEN: *(Rising)* Baby, cut loose from all that.

PEARL: *(Looks down at her arm)* Ain't no big thing, that's
just the deck I been dealt. Spades. Hand full of spades.
"Lucille?" Grannie Wade useta say to Momma: "Can't
we try and scrub off just a layer of that soot off the
child?" Lye soap. Stuff'd had my skin so raw for days
that I'd—never mind.

REUBEN: That's just ignorance.

PEARL: Don't mistake me. I've learned to be proud.

*(He stops cold, exits quickly, the sound of the shower turns
on he returns and holds her by the shoulders.)*

REUBEN: *(Pause)* If I had had me such a pretty little
girl—I'd—

PEARL: *(Interrupts)* See, in a way, it's like y'all can't
really help it.

REUBEN: What?

(She moves from him, paces.)

PEARL: Y'all get tempted. After all, everywhere you go
it's "Ms Anne" staring you down from somewhere.
Flaunted in ya face. *(Turning to exit with towel)*

REUBEN: Well. *(Pause)* Baby, you want ribs or catfish?

PEARL: *(Interrupts. Picks up a magazine from the vanity
table)* Even *Ebony*— *(Holding it up)* See here? Buttermilk

bright. Red-bone, high yella... Darkest they go is cinnamon-tan.

REUBEN: "Punkin", you know you the woman for me. Now, once and for all I don't give a damn 'bout...

PEARL: *(Whirling on him)* You don't get it, do you? It don't matter if you give a damn or don't give a damn—it's like the air you gotta breathe—you do gotta breathe, don't you? Well, DON'T YOU?

REUBEN: *(Carefully)* Of course I breathe.

PEARL: Well, then. And whether you "give a damn" 'bout air or don't give a damn, you breathing it. And your very life's depending on it breath by breath.

REUBEN: Honey, what the hell is all this about?

PEARL: Breathing! And how you and every other Colored man, every other man period can't help it. *(Grabbing the dress)* Where'd I first see this dress? Down at Hudsons. Draped tight on a mannequin pale as flour... *(Rushes to the dresser, holds up her toiletries one by one)* This lipstick. In a box with a face pink pale on the cover... This face powder in a tin with a face the shade of paper...

REUBEN: Pearl—

PEARL: ...This bar of soap...this bubble bath...this bra and panties...these stockings...

REUBEN: All right.

PEARL: What's "all right" about it? I can't even douche without a snow-white staring back at me...

REUBEN: What'd you want me to say, huh? This is just the way the world is, we don't make it.

PEARL: No. You don't. That's how come I cut you some slack. 'Cause we both know you men can't help it.

REUBEN: Pearl, when have you ever, ever known me to eye a white woman?

PEARL: If Marilyn Monroe ain't "white", then who is?

REUBEN: What else we gonna do? Stop watching movies? And when we get a T V it's gonna be the same thing. Why be miserable about it?

PEARL: When does "coal" get a chance to be wanted by the daddies in this world?

(He holds her.)

REUBEN: Listen—*(Pause)* I was a Daddy. *(Pause)* In my. Dream. A good, strong one. And our kids was all shades of—

PEARL: *(Interrupting, moving away)* Dreams. It may be a white man's world, but even a Colored Man gets to choose and pick us women. And deep down, deep way down, we both know you Colored men want us women as light as we can get. *(Pause)* Can't help but wanna sniff that "pale" pussy, can y'all?

REUBEN: I HAVE GIVEN YOU EVERYTHING. GONNA KEEP ON GIVING YOU EVERYTHING— *(Pause)* Don't I even go to that damn Church and get down on my knees and bow my head—

PEARL: *(fierce)* I SAW THAT PALE BITCH!! COME UP TO YOU. *(She considers a moment what to say next, then)* At the hotel.

REUBEN: *(Pause)* You think them women see "me"?! They see a nigga in a uniform to order around!

PEARL: I'm the one turning myself inside out. First I let myself love "blues" 'cause that's what you like. Now, I'm always hungry to get under the sheets! Forgetting to even say my prayers—just look at me! Can't get enough of ya!

(He grabs her)

REUBEN: You're the one keeping me steady, d'ya understand that!?

PEARL: Ever had yourself a "vanilla"?

REUBEN: *(Pause)* I was no monk "before" we met. I've never told you different. And they been all kinda shades, all right?

(PEARL studies him)

PEARL: The Sistahs point me out to they little girls in church: "Be like Sister Pearl. Be full of the Lord's Grace like Sister—I was a virgin when we met. *(Stops)* And there I stand. Singing to the glory of Jesus and underneath my robes the "cum" be running down.

REUBEN: *(Studies her)* How 'bout we get married this weekend. Why wait to afford the big, fancy—whatnot. Justice of the Peace. How 'bout it? *(PEARL reaches out and caresses Reuben's cheek)*

(Lights cross fade)

Scene Three

(Afternoon of the next day)

(Swirling lights, drum roll music—unseen announcer's booming voice)

UNSEEN ANNOUNCER: And now.... the moment we've all been waiting for... voted by popular demand, and taking over the title from Mr. and Mrs. Matthew Cleary of Akron, Ohio... Autorama 1957's COUPLE OF THE YEAR: Mister and Mrs Brian Syms of Fort Wayne, Indiana, let's give 'em a big hand folks!! Here they are crowned and winners of a brand, new 1958 Chev-ro-let!!!!!

(Loud crowd applause, "oohs" and "ahs".)

UNSEEN ANNOUNCER: We're told Mr. Syms is the legendary 'quota man', Salesman of the Year with his pretty Mrs.!! Congratulations, Mr. and Mrs.!!

(More applause)

*(*BRIAN *and* ZENA *seated inside an auto chassis, draped in the American flag. She holds a large trophy in her lap, they wave to the crowd, flashbulbs flash in their faces.)*

ZENA: Honey, smile, wave, honey...wave.

UNSEEN ANNOUNCER: Let's have a big kiss for the camera!

(In separate pool of light, REUBEN *dressed in his janitor's hotel uniform, sweeps and watches* BRIAN *and* ZENA.*)*

ZENA: Bri, whatsamatter?

BRIAN: Nothing. Wave.

ZENA: What's wrong?

(They pose again for the photo, beaming bright smiles, they kiss again. The band music starts up, swells, he offers his arm, they step out of the chassis, he takes her in his arms to the sound of crowd applause, they "waltz")

(Lights swirl, flare to brightness of flashbulbs, and then cross fade.)

Scene Four

(Lights up on PEARL. *She holds her wedding ring out with hope and pleasure, imagining she is wearing a "diamond". She playfully hums to* Wedding March *to herself, then as if answering a preacher.)*

PEARL: *(Blissfully)* "I do." *(Laughs to herself. Then points as if* REUBEN *were beside her)* "He does, too." *(She giggles, curls up, hugs herself, then spontaneously begins singing.)* ...We've come this far by faith

...Leaning on the Lord...
Trusting in his Holy Words
He's never failed me yet...
(She pauses, thinks. She eagerly pulls out REUBEN's *tattered guitar and begins to strum the cords. Her playing is terrible and she makes a playful face.)*

(She pauses, is about to put the guitar away, when she notices something stuck inside it. She eagerly pulls out the handkerchief, happy and assuming this is a "secret" present for herself. She unwraps the cloth and is at first confused and then shocked. She holds up the handkerchief with the baby hair tied with a tattered ribbon)

PEARL: *(Pause, suddenly laughing)* Well-well-well.
Have mercy on my soul. *(Pause) (Holding the hair)*
That lily-cow sure 'nough give him "a piece of her",
all right. Sure 'nough! *(Pause)* Face it. You buck up and
face it and don't you *dare* shed no tears! *(Pause)* You
ain't nothing but a "notch on the belt" for that Bastard.
You just another one of his "hens"—the "soot-colored
hen" in his "stable"—just keep on the leash for his thrill.
(Referring to the hair) "This"—this is "the truth" you
Bastard. *(Pause)* NO TEARS!! Stay proud. *(Pause)* I
thank you, oh Lord for this gift I have received. Just
guide me. Just guide me. Lord, I'm in your hands. Show
me the path I must take. A-men. A-men.

(Lights cross fade)

Scene Five

*(*BRIAN *and* ZENA's *hotel bedroom. They enter)*

ZENA: What've I done? What? What?

BRIAN: Sh-h-h-h-h, it's not you, how could it ever be
you. *(A moment)* You just rest.

ZENA: *(Flaring)* You've been preoccupied all evening—
now, what IS it?

BRIAN: *(Flaring)* Woman, I'm trying to do my level best
here, all right!

*(He stops apologetically, motions for her to come to him,
she doesn't move.)*

BRIAN: *(Trying to kiss her)* Pretty please?

ZENA: *(Pause)* With sugar on top?

(He sits on the side of the bed, she curls up between his legs)

BRIAN: Sorry. It's. Company stuff. Not you. Never,
ever you. Got that? Never you. *(He drinks.)*

ZENA: That's your third vodka in twenty
minutes..Please stop.

(He crosses over to the trophy, holding it up.)

BRIAN: "Indiana legend." "Couple of the Year."
"The Club."

ZENA: *(Holds up membership card)* In the "front door"
at last.

BRIAN: Soon as we get home I'm taking you to the new
Jimmy Stewart picture.

ZENA: "Home." It's all I'm asking out of life. Nothing
spectacular. Just to live peaceful.

BRIAN: Get home on Friday after a long week, help you
serve supper, both of us throw the kids in the bath, and
all of us pile into the king-sized bed on rainy Saturday
afternoons to watch—

ZENA: *(Smiling)* Westerns.

BRIAN: Sure! But, if you and the kids insist on the
"mushy stuff" then we'll— *(Moment)* There are just
things I'll have to. "Get used to." If I. Take the
promotion.

ZENA: What things, Brian?

(He starts waltzing her around the room)

BRIAN: Harvest Dance of '52. Gardenia in your hair.
First time for me in a tux. Didn't know that, did ya?

ZENA: My first ball gown. Ever. What things?

BRIAN: Never prayed inside so hard for somebody to
want to dance when I asked.

ZENA: I might not be able to.... What if something
happens—what if I can't carry to full term, what if—

BRIAN: *(Pause)* Jesus wouldn't let that happen to you.
Not after what you went through. Before "us." Loosing
your first family in one swipe.

ZENA: My girls were never baptized.

BRIAN: *(Waving this off)* Innocent is "innocent."
Now they're "heavenly angels." Can't be in "Limbo"
since you were Protestant back then, see.

ZENA: *(Pause)* Nothing's going to happen. God's
blessing us. Will you blame me, will you—No. Nothing
will happen. Yes. Yes!! *(Pause)* What Company "stuff."

BRIAN: *(Shakes head, then)* The factory tour. Some poor
bastard got his arm sliced clean off, right in front of me.

ZENA: Oh, that's all.

(He looks at her.)

ZENA: You know what I mean—It's not something with
us. *(Moment)* Tell me.

BRIAN: *(Shrugs)* Cries out, pisses, himself...

ZENA: Poor man.

BRIAN: *(Absentmindedly changing his suit jacket)* "You are
my lucky star..." *(Pause)* Funny...it's not as much blood
as you'd expect at first, 'cause the body goes into shock.

ZENA: He was treated right away I hope?

BRIAN: *(Nods)* Amazing. The sight of it...exposed bone...

ZENA: I've seen exposed bone. A man sliced off his foot in a tractor accident when I was little.

BRIAN: Then you know.

ZENA: It's yellow.

BRIAN: Not white. Who'd have thought, huh?

(She stands stock still)

BRIAN: Wen...honey? What's this in the bed? *(He holds up the snake-skin bag.)*

ZENA: *(A moment, then)* Ain't it—isn't it, cute.

BRIAN: Wendy?

ZENA: Must've spilled out of my shopping. Bag. There's this quaint little knickknack shop on Woodward Avenue—so I just—and it was so cheap. Reminded me of. Where I grew up.

BRIAN: *(Holding it up)* Well, it's certainly a conversation piece, I'll grant you that.

ZENA: Don't open it.

(He does. Pulls out the cross and squirrel tail)

BRIAN: What the be-Jesus...!

ZENA: Negroes and poor whites back down home in the back woods, call those things "Charms". For luck. *("Laughing")* Silly superstitions of poor, ignorant folks.

BRIAN: Not the poor, ignorant "folks," I knew. Catholics would have a field day over something so....

ZENA: *("charming")* "Primitive." Yes. *(Pause)* You know me with shopping, I just couldn't resist.

BRIAN: So, what'll we do with the thing.

(She takes the snake skin bag and cross out of his hands, flings it in the trash.)

ZENA: So much for nostalgia. *(Pause)* Whatever happens, we're gonna have that quiet life. Just us.

(Kissing him as they fall onto the bed)

Scene Six

(Next morning)

(The basement: darkness, LLOYD and BRIAN enter, each carries a bright flashlight with an air of furtiveness.)

LLOYD: Morning, Mister Syms. C'mon.

(They glance around for a beat, then:)

BRIAN: Sir, Lloyd, should we even be down here?

LLOYD: *(Referring to this flashlight)* You're about to carry out a vital tactical maneuver for Patterson, "Inc", son. Be proud.

BRIAN: Sneaking around down here in the basement.

LLOYD: *(Using his flashlight to look around)* This here'll do for a "look-out". *(Pause, studies BRIAN)* You were in the infantry, right? Right?

BRIAN: Of course.

LLOYD: *(Salutes)* And when orders came down from "high command" what did you do? *(Pause)* What did you do?

BRIAN: The "war" was the "war." Here we're all supposed to be working for the same team.

LLOYD: Exactly. Precisely! You tell that to whoever's double-crossing us with our competitors, boy. You tell that to whoever's been leaking these "sissy" Interoffice *(Mocking)* "Safety Memos" to middle management—

coast to coast! Next thing you know we'll have the rank and file, AND their union pitching fits! You want that? You want our profit margins to nose dive just 'cause some "village idiot" may or may not have tightened the screws on a couple of brakes?!

(BRIAN *is silent.*)

LLOYD: Brian?

BRIAN: *(Trying to lighten up)* It's just that I feel like "Bogie" in the *Maltese Falcon*.

*(*LLOYD *laughs along then is deadly serious.)*

LLOYD: There's a "cabal" of cowards in our ranks!

(The sound of a freight elevator, LLOYD *and* BRIAN *crouch low.)*

LLOYD: Well, well, well. Rogerson...

BRIAN: And Taylor.

LLOYD: *(Delighted)* Klein's men! Klein! *Knew* he never should've been promoted to Senior V P, I *warned* the "top brass." Ha. *(Pause)* Ready for your shootout with Myers this afternoon?

BRIAN: Ready.

LLOYD: Let's see you come at out with both "barrels loaded". You ace the sales presentation, then the *coup de grace*—we present names of these yellow traitors— *(Offers a pad and pencil to* BRIAN*)* Touchdown!

BRIAN: What happens if it doesn't stop? I mean, say we put those '58s on the road—

LLOYD: *(Checking his watch)* Senior V P lunch. You keep an eye on that door, bring me a "who's who" of everybody coming in or going out. Meet back at my suite at "fourteen-hundred" hours.

BRIAN: Yes, Sir. Lloyd.

(LLOYD *pats* BRIAN *on the back as exits, he starts out, stops, delighted.)*

LLOYD: Klein!

(LLOYD *exits.* BRIAN *begrudgingly scribbles down the names on his pad, then stops, tears off paper, crumbles it.)*

BRIAN: Christ. *(Stops himself, smoothes the paper back out and continues to write.)*

(A beat. Lights up stronger, REUBEN *appears with this pail and mop, humming blues casually to himself.* REUBEN *enters his broom closet.* BRIAN *quickly hides in the shadows and is about to exit, when:)*

(A beat. ZENA *appears from the shadows.* BRIAN *does as double take, so astonished he nearly calls out, nearly dropping his flashlight. He watches as she approaches* REUBEN's *broom closet.)*

(BRIAN *is astonished and hides in the shadows.)*

REUBEN: What the—hell—

(REUBEN *quickly gets out his keys—they look around,* BRIAN *ducks into shadows as if in a corner,* REUBEN *motions her into the supply closet)*

REUBEN: Shit, Zena my job!

ZENA: *(Angry)* Hell with—you're just down here to get more soap or rags or whatever—lock the door.

REUBEN: What the hell—you coming down here like this! Dammit!

ZENA: *("mocking", batting her eyes)* Me? Anybody ask me, I got "lost."

REUBEN: Get outta here 'fore I get in trouble!

(ZENA *holds up snake skin bag.)*

ZENA: Trouble!! "Trouble"!! I trusted you. Trusted you to act decent but, no—no!

REUBEN: What!!? What??!!

ZENA: Don't play dumb.

REUBEN: Talk sense.

ZENA: What was this doing in my hotel room last night!
Doing in my bed!!

REUBEN: Don't ask me! You the one threw it back into
the— *(Stops)*

(ZENA starts to go for his face.)

ZENA: Liar! Liar!

(He holds her by shoulders)

REUBEN: Why would I act the devil towards you?!
Ain't you give me the keepsake from our little girls?

ZENA: Well, then how—who—

(REUBEN holds the bag, stunned.)

REUBEN: Goddamn. *(Pause)* Pearl.

ZENA: Your lady?

REUBEN: Fiancé.

ZENA: How'd she come to get a hold of this.

REUBEN: Don't you think I'm trying to figure?

ZENA: Don't tell me she's a "maid" in this place?!
Oh, gawd.

REUBEN: No need to "raise the devil", I'll take care of it.

ZENA: She knows all about us?! Don't she?! You just
couldn't leave well enough alone.

REUBEN: Yeah, I'm just that type of "fool"! So proud of
how I messed up our family that I brag about it every
day??!! *(Pause)* After all, women just LOVE the smell of
failure on a man. Huh, Zena?

ZENA: Why'd we cross paths. In the first place?
What's the -what's the hex on us—what's the

REUBEN: Quit that foolishness. All that
back-down-home mess.

ZENA: What's the "sign" we supposed to be finding
in all this?

REUBEN: Quit! All that ole Geechee stuff's passed you,
now, wiped "clean".

ZENA: Yes. Yes. "Clean."

REUBEN: Zena, looka here. This time next week, you'll
be back home. This place'll be long since passed outta
your mind—and—and I'll be a new married man.

ZENA: *(She mimes tipping a man's hat)* "Ma'am, you want
the car that's reserved for our white clientele, right this
way. Right this way." *(Laughs)*. *(Pause)* Taking my new
"seat" for the first time. Surrounded by all of them.
Me, listening, watching, trembling. Miles and miles of
"listening and watching." *(Pause)* Hands folded neat in
my lap. I almost bolted, almost "told" on myself, almost
ran "back." *(Pause)* You think I'm terrible, don't you.

REUBEN: I'm to judge? *(Pause)* 'Sides, everybody's gotta
"season they own soup." *(Pause)* How'd you learn to
speak so—

ZENA: Rooming houses. Slop-jobs taken to stay alive.
Working my way up to "waitress," finally. Radio.
Listening. Practicing. Night school. Getting up the guts
to cross through that door.

REUBEN: You never wanted for guts. No.

ZENA: We already know that the "poor" white folks
are really no different from "us", 'cept for that badge
of "color" they cling to. And the rich ones...still got
the same flesh and blood hopes and dreams and
nightmares like everybody else. *(Pause)* What's the sin

in wanting more out of the itty-bitty slice that life has handed over. *(Pause)* I gotta get going, I gotta—I gotta. Take it easy that's all.

REUBEN: Maybe you better go lay down.

ZENA: Nunno. I've got to...I've got to... *(Pause)* Ha. Two days from now, I'm back in my own kitchen, my own garden out back... *(Pause)* Maybe. There'll come a time when— *(Holds out her arm, indicating her color)* "This" really won't count for nothing. *(Pause)* Fat chance.

REUBEN: Let it 'lone, honey.

ZENA: You try walking around inside flesh that people either worship or despise—and *then* tell me to leave it alone.

REUBEN: Oh, Zee

ZENA: *(To herself and him)* But, *nobody* dare slam a door in my face, now! And now the world's filled with folks hoping and praying that I'll wave 'em over to my table.

REUBEN: It was the way you throw your head back and laugh. The way you walk bold in the world—that's what. I. First come after. *(Pause, indicating her skin color)* This weren't nothing to me.

(A silence as they stare at each other. He reaches for her slowly)

REUBEN: Your earring's coming out.

(He helps her fix it. They stare)

(REUBEN steps off the platform, BRIAN looks on from the shadows. ZENA steps down as lights cross fade.)

Scene Seven

(Afternoon)

*(*BRIAN *and* ZENA*'s hotel room)*

(Someone smoking in the dark—the shadow of a figure, the person's back to the audience. The figure flicks a cigarette lighter on and off.)

(On the other side of the stage SISTER NICODEMOS *enters carrying the flaming glass bowl in her hands,* ZENA *behind her.* SISTER NICODEMOS *sets down the bowl, takes flour from her apron pocket, douses the flame. Holds the bowl up to the light)*

SISTER NICODEMOS: Oke-dokee-lemme read the pattern here.

ZENA: Yes? Well? How many times do I have to come 'fore you can "see" what it is?

SISTER NICODEMOS: *(Pause)* I see... "girl" —most definitely, girl. There's a daughter coming to you.

ZENA: Finally. Pale? Pale, right? Is she pale?

SISTER NICODEMOS: 'Course she'll be "born" pale, but will she "stay" pale....

ZENA: Do you see yellow? Or darker. What?! What?!

*(*REUBEN *enters on his side of the stage walks into the light, calling out:)*

REUBEN: Pearl!! PEARL!!

SISTER NICODEMOS: *(To* ZENA*)* Calm yourself. Of course, ya momma pale.

ZENA: They say high yellow like me, they say my Daddy—who knows—of course he was some white "pole-catting" bastard.

SISTER NICODEMOS: I'm sorry.

ZENA: Don't give me "sorry." Don't need your "sorry". Got a sweet man at home, a lovely house where I live. When I leave here I cab right downtown to a honeymoon suite in the Hilton.

SISTER NICODEMOS: Only way a Colored get in there is to be carrying a broom.

ZENA: I didn't come here to "moan" about our folks. What can you tell me!!!

SISTER NICODEMOS: The truth! But, something's blocking my view. Look, ain't gonna lie. The pattern's neither this way nor that way on it.

REUBEN: Pearl!? *(He sees something, goes to it, reaches down, it's his broken guitar. He holds up the found handkerchief with the baby hair. He runs out, panicked.)*

(On her side of the stage, ZENA holds up the cross with the squirrel tail on it.)

ZENA: This what I get for believing in stupid superstition!! Silly, charms and whatnot!

SISTER NICODEMOS: Your momma could come through this girl—Your grannie-momma could come through this girl. Or your great, or great-great.

ZENA: *(More desperate)* Can you see that far back? Can you see *any* dark ghosts hovering? How many generations can the dark creep up to, can it show up in the generations to come!? Tell me!!! WHERE IS THE MAGIC IN THIS WORLD—burn more!! Try it again!!

SISTER NICODEMOS: Zena, take it easy. Maybe the Spirits don't *want* us to know.

ZENA: You saw my twins without me having to tell you nothing. See this, then!! I've got one more day left— gimme another appointment!! "See" —Burn. "Burn more"!!

(SISTER NICODEMOS exits, ZENA crosses into the other side of stage where the figure sits smoking.)

Scene Eight

ZENA: Bri? Honey? Why aren't you dressed yet, Sweetheart?

(Lights up. BRIAN rises, he is drinking heavily, smoking. He continues to flick his cigarette lighter on and off.)

ZENA: Darling? Sweetie?

BRIAN: Drink?

(He moves over to small table, pours scotch in shot glass, holds it out to her)

ZENA: Whatsamatter?

BRIAN: *(Quietly)* You'd better have a drink.

ZENA: I don't want a drink.

BRIAN: You'd better have a drink.

ZENA: Brian—?

BRIAN: Where's that "cross" thing-a-ma-gig? Thing?

ZENA: What?

BRIAN: The cross with the squirrel thing—get it. *(Silence. Then)* GET IT GET IT!!! GET IT!!

ZENA: WHO'D YOU THINK YOU'RE TALKING TO, MISTER!?

(He starts towards her, she, bewildered, pulls out the cross with the squirrel tail attached starts to bring it to him.)

BRIAN: Don't come close to me.

(She stops. She tosses it to him, he catches it)

ZENA: What's happened? Whatever it is, Beloved, we can—

(Pause. He holds up the cross.)

BRIAN: Now, give me your hand—your ring finger, your diamond finger.

(She quizzically offers her hand, he takes it softly, kissing her hand, then squeezes.)

ZENA: You're hurting me—Brian—!

(He takes his cigarette lighter and holding her hand, brings it closer and closer to her, she tries to pull away, but can't, then finally he let's her go)

ZENA: *(Lethal)* Don't you EVER, EVER, EVER—!!

BRIAN: But, the cross will protect you, Darling. This nigger charm will make sure it won't hurt. Let's see, now—how to work it? Hum? HUM? Do we kneel down and what—smell it? Lick it! Wave it! WHAT!! WHAT!!! *(Suddenly shushes himself)* Sh-h-h-h-h-h. Can't have shouts heard coming from the "Honeymoon Suite"—after all, we're the "Autorama Couple of 1958!" We have been crowned, coronated!

ZENA: "Crown" or no "crown"—I did *not* haul myself up all the way out of Mississippi just to spend my life with a drunk!

BRIAN: Did you fuck niggers back down in "ole Misssss-sppye" too?

(ZENA stops, stunned)

BRIAN: KNEEL DOWN! KNEEL!

(He rushes at her, she tries to escape, is stunned, he holds her firmly, grips her, pushes her to the floor)

BRIAN: "Hail Mary, full of grace, the Lord is with you, blessed art thou among women and blessed is the fruit of they womb, Jesus..."

(He realizes she is crying. He holds her gently, hugs her)

BRIAN: Help me to "wake up" from this—Just a nightmare, Bri Syms, "wake up you bastard, wake up!" *(Pause)* That wasn't you, that was some—somebody else! Couldn't have been *my* beloved, no! Not the women I hold above all others, not the mother of my child—
sneaking out of closets followed by a nigger man! Sneaking 'round like a thief—sneaking 'round like a common slut on the street— *(Stops)* Tell me to wake up!

(She rises instantly, moves away. Gazes out. A long silence)

ZENA: He never touched me. He's. Someone. I once knew.

BRIAN: "Knew", how?

ZENA: From back home. Grew up with.

BRIAN: "Knew"?

ZENA: No idea he'd was here till I saw him—first night we got here.

BRIAN: "KNEW"—Let's get back to "knew" — in what sense, "knew".

ZENA: You saw me this afternoon? What were you doing in the basement?

BRIAN: In what goddamn sense, "knew"?!

ZENA: *(Quietly)* Oh, you think that's the worst thing that could happen?

BRIAN: You're a pregnant woman, for fuck-sake! Jesus Christ!

ZENA: He's my husband, Reu— *(Correcting herself)* Brian.

(Silence)

BRIAN: You. You told me you were a widow.

ZENA: Back then he was a drunk. It was unbearable. Our baby girls died, it really was "flu". WAS *NEVER* SUPPOSED TO SEE HIM AGAIN IN LIFE.

BRIAN: Great Goddamn, Jesus, God. Life's not supposed to be like the movies, goddammit, the "movies" are supposed to be like the "movies". I'm—I'm—I'm— *(Stops himself)* So. Now, you're married. Still. And to a Colored man. A white woman? These things happen down South? Is "Wendy" even your real name?

ZENA: *(Pause)* I'm a Colored woman, Brian.

(Silence. He bursts out laughing.)

BRIAN: Don't be ridiculous.

(A buzzer sounds, jolting them.)

*(*BRIAN *exits to the door, a beat, muffled voices—* LLOYD *appears.)*

LLOYD: Sorry, folks, sorry to bust in on the love nest. Business, dear lady—petty business.

*(*LLOYD *kisses* ZENA's *hand.)*

ZENA: Lloyd. Why don't I leave you two, to—

LLOYD: Nunno, you should hear this, Wendy. This is an "S O S". Fact is, Brian, your presentation was—merely adequate. What the hell were you so stiff in the lip about—you'd have thought you had a rod up your ass—! *(Quickly to* ZENA*)* Excuse me, pardon me, dear lady. Madeline would slap my hands. *(Pause)* "The Brass" is still on the fence about you versus that Myers sonofabitch—however—your tip on the "secret basement conferences" has worked in your favor, so that's at least—Now, tonight, at the dinner dance— Wendy, you'll be meeting the three C E Os who hold your husband's future in their hands. We all know Myers' wife is a— *(Pause)* well, she's not been as favored in the "looks department" as our dazzling, ever so charming—

ZENA: My gawd.

LLOYD: Sorry?

BRIAN: She's a little faint.

LLOYD: Ah, well, I'll be out of your way. Rest up for tonight. Wendy, we're counting on you to pull our guy over the goal line! *(He starts to exit, comes back, kisses* ZENA*'s hand, then)* Oh, and Syms—"light" on the booze, Boy. "Light."

*(*LLOYD *exits.* BRIAN *and* ZENA *stand still across from each other, silence. They both finish dressing.)*

BRIAN: What's your name. Your real name.

ZENA: Zena. Zena Sinclair.

BRIAN: Who? But—you're my lawful, wedded... *(He stops.)* How could you "be" a—and look so—

ZENA: You can't be that naive, Brian.

BRIAN: Stop acting so goddamn calm about it!

ZENA: This is how I look when I'm "caught". My Darling. But you wouldn't know—will never have a burden on your conscience that you carry to the grave.

BRIAN: *(Softly to himself)* You think not?

*(*REUBEN *is heard in the shadows)*

REUBEN: *(Calling out)* No secrets no more, Pearl!!!! Pearl!!??

*(*BRIAN *stiffly motions for* ZENA *to take his arm)*

BRIAN: You coming?

(Lights cross-fade.)

Scene Nine

(The party—Music, swirling lights, same as beginning of play. ZENA and BRIAN slip into formal wear right in front of the audience and while staring at each other in silence.)

(Lights change, the noise and of a ballroom crowd. ZENA and BRIAN stand side by side, "smiling", shaking hands, laughing. Both circle the room in separate conversations with unseen individuals. LLOYD is nearby, also shaking hands, watching them with approval.)

ZENA: ...*Monopoly*, not for me, all that money-grubbing. Ha. Now, *Scrabble*—not only fun, but improves vocabulary... *(Nods)* Exactly! That's my point!

BRIAN: ...Mickey Mantle's the only switch-hitter I've ever seen with so much power from each side of the plate.

ZENA: ...Mister Dennison, did I hear you say, *The King and I*? Excellent family entertainment.

BRIAN: ...Mantle for me. Mantle all the way.

LLOYD: *(To unseen person, pointing to BRIAN and ZENA)* ...Those two at the helm of the younger generation, boys—those two at the helm... *(laughing)* Our sales'll sky-rocket. And watch that "Mrs" of his take over the Club!

(The band music starts up. Benny Goodman's: Sentimental Journey. *BRIAN and ZENA automatically lock arms and swing into a waltz.)*

BRIAN: So, you used me, then.

ZENA: Oh, certainly. Seven years of—of cheering you, soothing you, wrapping you in my—oh, yes—and carrying your child. Showing up here, keeping "this" going—No love, of course—just.

BRIAN: What'd you expect me to think?

ZENA: I expect—nothing. I expect nothing.

(Dancing continues, suddenly everyone freezes in place.)

(ZENA steps into the spotlight, facing us.)

ZENA: God can slip a "test" right in-between your breath and you not even know it. *(pause, to audience)* There is an impostor among you. I can feed on lies, and more lies, and live very well. Oh, yes. *(Pause)* WATCH OUT!! LOCK THE GATES, SHUT THE WINDOWS! *(Pause)* "Snow" is falling through the cracks!

(ETTA appears to ZENA. She throws off her necklace of bones, scattering it to the floor. ZENA smiles at her and nods. She looks over the audience,)

ZENA: *(To herself referring to the audience as if we are a crowd. She looks over her flesh, caresses her face)* Don't blame "them" for what you won't love *yourself, (Pause)* "Snow".

(On another side of the stage, REUBEN appears, banging on a door.)

REUBEN: *(banging on a door)* Pearl! Pearl Henderson!

(A voice calls out:)

UNSEEN VOICE: She done moved out, Mister. Left no forwarding address.

(PEARL appears in a spotlight, dressed in a bright red choir robe, with a tambourine. She calls out into the air, jubilantly. Sounds of a clapping, church congregation are heard.)

PEARL: *(smiling, raising her arms on high)* Hallelujah!! Bless his Holy name, Church, A-men! *(Pause)* Church, I had a *secret*, Lord ha'mercy, Hallelujah!

VOICES: A-men! Hallelujah!

PEARL: Jesus caught me living a "double-dealing" lie!!

VOICES: Preach!! PREACH!!

PEARL: Yessir. *(Points to her brow)* See, up here's where the Devil can snare ya!!

VOICES: AMEN! PRAISE HIS HOLY NAME!

PEARL: *(Smiling, clapping)* I had fallen by the way-side. Was living inside out, and "double-sided"! Can I getta witness!

VOICES: TALK!! TALK!

PEARL: But, Praise God, Je-sus took me back!

VOICES: Hallelujah! Preach it, Sistah!! A-MEN! A-MEN!!

PEARL: Can I get a witness, ha'mercy, Je-sus! Jesus say, "Pearl!?"

VOICES: "Pearl"!!!??

PEARL: "Pearl"!!!??

VOICES: "Pearl!!!??"

PEARL: "Pearl! Come on back 'home'. Come on back to what's true and *real* in ya, Pearl!" And now, I love myself and my God—Praise Him, Hallelujah!

(Clapping. Lights fade on PEARL.)

Scene Ten

(BRIAN and ZENA enter their hotel room. He whips off his tie.)

ZENA: Congratulations.

BRIAN: "Executive Director of Regional Sales."

ZENA: Yes.

BRIAN: We were a "smash".

ZENA: "Brian and Wendy Syms," the couple to be "seen" with, the people to "know".

BRIAN: I know you love me, I believe that.

ZENA: Do you, Brian? Do you?

BRIAN: Wen—Zena. You've got to understand— this is all—this is—

ZENA: I never set out. It wasn't like that. Me setting out to find somebody to lay hold of. Somebody to "use".

BRIAN: I've got things to get used to here.

ZENA: When we met...

BRIAN: When we "met", I thought the goddamn "leprechauns" had finally pulled my name out of the "hat".

ZENA: I thought to myself, "so, this is what it feels like to look forward to the day ahead."

BRIAN: What I wanna know is.

ZENA: And I was still counting tips to barely make the rent and watching the movies so careful to learn how to "stand" and "walk", and how to "handle myself" and here we are, now. A "smash".

BRIAN: What I wanna know is—how could you—how—how—

ZENA: Tell a "half-truth" and live with it, and have it grow a good, firm, tough, "skin"? Stay with "Patterson Inc." long enough, you'll find out.

BRIAN: Look, I'm not "pointing fingers", I'm just—

ZENA: (Acknowledging his meaning) Yes. Yes. Yes.

BRIAN: "Marry me." I said. "Widow," you said. You said, "barren".

ZENA: "Barren" was what I had been told to believe.

BRIAN: I figure, here's the woman whom I "fit." We are a "fit." We love each other. We "fit". "A family"? Well, there're one or two orphans in this world that'll need us, what the hell.

ZENA: Carrying our child.

BRIAN: Goddammit, the surprise of "that," the joy— the goddammit "hallelujah" of that has held me up out of the "muck" these last few days.

ZENA: We can figure everything else out, once we get back home. Right?

BRIAN: Home. Yes.

ZENA: All I want is to live peaceful!!

BRIAN: We were a triumph tonight.

ZENA: Let's just figure it all back home.

BRIAN: Hell, America's made of folks who make themselves up every hour of every day. Why should "we" be any different from anyone else.

ZENA: "Any different from anyone else," Brian?

BRIAN: Look, whatever the baby—after all "he", "she" is half me.

ZENA: Yes.

BRIAN: And you. You must have—

ZENA: Don't say it—! Don't "jinx" it!

BRIAN: ...more white in you than anything else. Nobody can tell about you.

ZENA: DON'T SAY IT, DON'T SAY IT OUT LOUD!!

BRIAN: WHAT??! WHAT??! SOMEBODY'S GOTTA "SAY" IT!

ZENA: It won't rest on us, huh?

BRIAN: What? What?

ZENA: What'd I "do" about Zena, now.

BRIAN: Once we get back home, like you say, we'll—.

ZENA: What'd I "do" about Zena, now,Brian?

BRIAN: Will you just take it easy? Like you say, nothing needs to be "rushed into" tonight.

ZENA: Answer.

BRIAN: You heard what I said.

ZENA: What'd we do? "Send me off someplace when I'm full-term"? Then, "wait" to see how the "score" turns out?

BRIAN: Oh, make me sound crude, go ahead. Just what were you thinking of doing "just in case" anyway? *(Pause)* Before I stumbled onto you, *(Mocking, enraged)* "What if I can't carry to term, Darling."

ZENA: So. "This" is who we really are to each other, then.

BRIAN: Angel...

ZENA: WE CAN'T MAKE THE FAIRY TAKE WORK. WE CAN'T FOLD IT, END IT, MAKE IT "FIT".

BRIAN: Wendy, give us time. Please.

ZENA: No, need to send me any money.

BRIAN: NOW HOLD UP HERE. Stop. No. Yesterday, I'm told I'm gonna be spending my life selling "white elephants" to the unsuspecting public, and today, today—my "family", my "home" goes up in big "puff" —NO!!! *(Pause)* No child of mine is gonna have to put up with what I had to live through. "Bad food," and "no" food, and leaking ceilings, and third class rooming houses with cabbage stinking up the piss-soaked, hand-me-down-play-pen in the center of the room. *(Pause)* I live just to walk in the door and catch a whiff of your perfume!

ZENA: Tell me what to *do*. Answer.

BRIAN: If its. If it turns out. We'd make sure it gets a good home. The right home.

(ZENA *begins to pack what appears to be only essential items into a suitcase*)

BRIAN: Zena—Wendy! Where're you running off to?

ZENA: That's what's got me shaking all over.

BRIAN: You're not doing this! No!

ZENA: Help me so I can stay then! (*Silence*) Some. Colored women have had to raise their children alone for generations.

BRIAN: You're not a—

ZENA: And then our grandkids and the "speck" of dust? Do we "sweat" over each and every "new Syms" that draws breath, Bri? TELL ME.

(BRIAN *is silent as* ZENA *faces him, then exits, suitcase in hand.*)

BRIAN: Wait.

(PEARL *appears in spotlight, stomping to gospel music. Addressing us*)

PEARL: Who out there among ya got secrets eating ya, up! C'mon to Je-sus!! Hallelujah! C'mon! (*She stands in her own spotlight*)

(ZENA *stands in her own spotlight*. ETTA *appears to* ZENA. ETTA *throws down her necklace of bones.*)

ETTA: Which way now, "Snow"?

(*Slowly,* ZENA *picks up the necklace, draping it around herself.*)

ZENA: (*Pause*) "Zena-Marie Sinclair". (*Pause*) Which way, now?

(A train whistle blows.)

*(*REUBEN *stands in a spotlight. He pulls out an unopened whiskey bottle, from a bag, holding it up to the light, then firmly sets the bottle down, backing away from it.)*

REUBEN: Man, it's up to you. You gonna break?! Gonna shake hands with that Devil? What you gonna do?

(A train CONDUCTOR *calls out from the darkness)*

CONDUCTOR: *(Offstage)* Attention, please. The "Silverline Midnight Express" to Chicago, making connections in Chicago for Denver and on to San Diego! Leaving from track 77. ALL ABOARD. TICKETS, PLEASE!! TICKETS!!!

(Lights up on REUBEN, PEARL, BRIAN. BRIAN *is straightening his tie, trying with effort to face the world alone.)*

REUBEN: PEARL!!

BRIAN: ZENA!!

(Then lights down on the others as ZENA *stands in spotlight alone. She reaches out, a train ticket in hand,)*

ZENA: *(Hopeful, resolute)* Just keep on looking for a "sign", Zena-Marie. Yes. Just keep on looking for a "sign"! *(Blackout)*

END OF PLAY

www.ingramcontent.com/pod-product-compliance
Lightning Source LLC
Chambersburg PA
CBHW052200090426

42741CB00010B/2351